St Patrick

Alf McCreary

First published in 2009 by
Appletree Press Ltd
The Old Potato Station
14 Howard Street South
Belfast BT7 1AP

Tel: + 44 (28) 90 24 30 74
Fax: + 44 (28) 90 24 67 56
Email: reception@appletree.ie
Web-site: www.appletree.ie

Text by Alf McCreary
Illustrations by Ann MacDuff (pp 4 and 58)

Additional photographic credits as credited on p128

First published in 2006 as *In St Patrick's Footsteps* by Appletree Press

A catalogue record for this book is available from the British Library.

St Patrick

ISBN: 978 1 84758 117 4

Desk & Marketing Editor: Jean Brown
Editorial Work: Jim Black
Designer: Stuart Wilkinson
Production Manager: Paul McAvoy

9 8 7 6 5 4 3 2 1

AP3596

Contents

Introduction

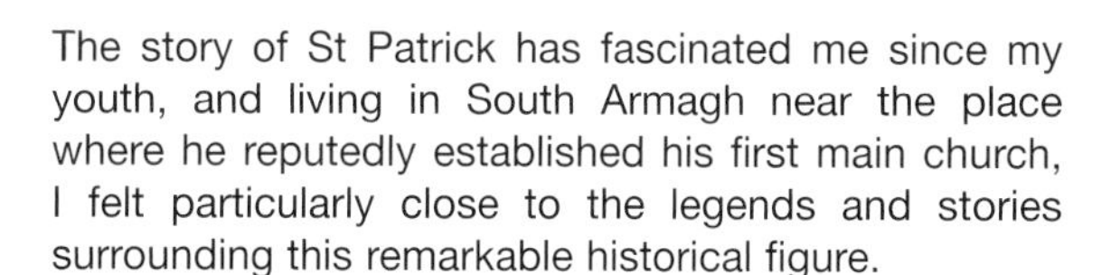

The story of St Patrick has fascinated me since my youth, and living in South Armagh near the place where he reputedly established his first main church, I felt particularly close to the legends and stories surrounding this remarkable historical figure.

Some years ago, I wrote a major history of Armagh city, and during my extensive research I read widely about the history of St Patrick, and particularly his autobiographical Confessio which provides us with a sketchy but intimate and yet historically reliable self-portrait of the man and his mission.

While researching and writing this present volume, I have attempted to stay with the known facts of his life and journeys, but I have also been enriched in my understanding of that remarkable and holy man by the sheer range and depth of the folklore and legends associated with his name.

Rather than taking away from the story of St Patrick, I found that they actually added to it, and between these lines I hope you will share with me a vivid and inspiring picture of an early Christian and a person of remarkable courage and conviction who became deservedly the Patron Saint of Ireland.

– Alf McCreary

Statue of Saint Patrick, Slieve Patrick, Co. Down

The Life of St Patrick

Although the name of St Patrick is well known in history, and it is famous throughout the world, very little is known of the man himself. His story is steeped in legends and myths which themselves have formed a tradition about Ireland's Patron Saint and have taken on a life and a reality of their own. If Patrick had visited every place in Ireland associated with his name, he would have had no time to rest – even if he had indeed lived to be 120 years of age, as so colourfully claimed by the 7th-century Irish scribe and priest known as Muirchu.

However, a more recent historian, the late Bishop R.P.C. Hanson, pointed out that while it was impossible to map out accurately the saint's supposed movements in Ireland, a much later tradition and custom "may have hallowed these places. This is not to say, of course, that all authentic memory of Patrick died out soon after his death."

It is believed, however, that by the time Patrick arrived on his mission, there were already Christians in Ireland. It is recorded as early as 431 AD that Pope Celestine had sent a man called Palladius to work in an area thought to be around Leinster, and he almost certainly would have had a number of colleagues. However Patrick makes no mention of any immediate predecessor, and although he may not have been the first Christian missionary to come to Ireland, he certainly became the most famous.

By far the most reliable account of Patrick's life, though in places sketchy, is his autobiography titled *Confessio*. It was written in rudimentary Latin in the 5th century, near the end of his life when he was, for those times, a comparatively old man. Somewhat earlier he had also written his *Letter To Coroticus*, which was a fierce condemnation of a war-lord who had carried into captivity a large number of young converts whom Patrick had baptised only the day before.

His autobiography, however, is full of Christian energy and zeal, and it has a remarkable humility which testifies to the saintly nature of this holy, yet tough and worldly-wise man. Its tone is set by the very first words "I am Patrick, a sinner, most unlearned, the least of all the faithful, and utterly despised by many."

Patrick tells us that his father was called Calpornius, and that his grandfather Potitus was a priest. He further relates that they lived in the village of *Bannavem Taburnilae*, and that it was from there that he was taken captive and carried off as a slave to Ireland "with many thousands of people."

Unfortunately, no one knows exactly where he was captured, in what was then Roman Britain. There is speculation about several places, including the modern equivalents of South Wales, the north-east coast of England, and Kilpatrick in Scotland. It is most likely, however, that Patrick lived somewhere on the west coast, which would have been the most easily accessible to Irish slavers.

Patrick tells us that he spent six years in captivity herding sheep in all winds and weathers, including "snow, frost and rain". It is popularly supposed that he spent this period in the north of Ireland at Slemish, near Ballymena. During this period he became a strong Christian convert and says that "in a single day I would say as many as a hundred prayers, and almost as many in the night."

He was told in a dream that he would escape, and accordingly he travelled some 200 miles to an unknown port, perhaps near Waterford, where he boarded a ship which was leaving Ireland. After many adventures, including intense hunger and further captivity thought to be on mainland Europe, he returned again to his parents in Britain. He then had another vivid dream where a man called Victoricus asked him to return to Ireland "and walk among us once more." He obeyed the call, and went back to Ireland as an ordained Bishop to carry out his mission among the people. He is thought to have made his headquarters in what is modern Armagh, near the seat of political power in his time, and there he established his first main church in or around 445 AD.

There was then a further shift of political power towards the east of the Province of Ulster, and Patrick is said to have died in the area of Downpatrick, near Saul, where he is reputed to have arrived in Ireland on his saintly mission. He is also thought to have been buried at a site adjacent to the Church of Ireland Cathedral in Downpatrick. According to one legend, Patrick's disciples placed his body on a cart pulled by white oxen, and the place where they eventually stayed at rest marked the site of his grave.

Patrick died on 17 March in 460 AD, and the tradition of observing that date world-wide as St Patrick's Day stretches back to at least the 7th century. The scribe Muirchu claims that darkness was suspended for 12 days, that angels singing psalms kept a vigil over Patrick's body for the first night, and that he lived to be 120 – just like some of the Old Testament Patriarchs!

The literature of early Ireland is filled with such claims about Patrick's life and death, including the priceless 9th-century *Book of Armagh*, written by the Master

Scribe Ferdomnach, and containing Muirchu's *Life of Patrick*, and another life of the saint by Bishop Tirechan, who adds to the speculation. He claimed that Patrick ordained some 350 bishops and that he travelled round Ireland, founding churches and performing miracles.

A much later writer James Stuart, whose seminal *Historical Memoirs of Armagh* was published in 1819, drew on many sources available since the publication of the original *Book of Armagh*. He claimed that Patrick had been to many places in Ireland – including Dublin, Wexford, Cashel, Mayo, Donegal, Coleraine and, of course, Armagh.

Given the scant historical evidence available, this is as difficult to disprove as it is to verify. It is worth noting, however, that the late Cardinal Tomas O'Fiaich, a respected historian, concluded that most of Patrick's missionary work took place "north of a line running from Galway to Wexford. Most of the churches which claimed Patrick as their founder are situated in this half of the country."

What is clear, however, is that Patrick was a most successful missionary who established a solid base for the kind of Christianity which gave Ireland an early reputation as 'the island of saints and scholars'. Though it cannot be said with authority that every site associated with Patrick's name was visited by the saint, it is clear that generations of prayer and worship in these places gave them a truly Patrician spirit.

It is in this spirit that we set out upon our journey in St Patrick's footsteps, including Armagh and the two great cathedrals which bear his name, Slemish in Co. Antrim and Downpatrick, as well as Donegal, Mayo, Dublin and elsewhere. In his *Confessio* Patrick writes "It was most necessary to spread our nets so that a great multitude and throng might be caught for God, and that there be clerics everywhere to baptise and exhort a people in need and want..."

Our journey, more than 1,500 years later, will try to retrace the surer and better-known of those saintly footsteps.

"IT WAS MOST NECESSARY TO SPREAD OUR NETS SO THAT A GREAT MULTITUDE AND THRONG MIGHT BE CAUGHT FOR GOD."

-ST PATRICK

Interior of St Patrick's Church of Ireland Cathedral, Armagh

Armagh City

Armagh is widely regarded as the ecclesiastical capital of Ireland and is reputed to be the place where St Patrick established his first main church in the year 445 AD. The city has two great cathedrals named after him, as well as two important libraries, a comprehensive museum, an impressive exhibition and educational centre at St Patrick's Trian, and also the nearby Navan Fort and Visitor Centre which features the history of the ancient Kings of Ulster.

The Church of Ireland Cathedral is situated on a steep hill known as Sallow Ridge (known in Gaelic as *Druim Saileach*) where Patrick is said to have built his first stone church. This is also the resting-place of Brian Boru, the High-King of Ireland who was killed at the Battle of Clontarf in 1014. This victory was the beginning of the end of the Viking domination of Ireland, and Brian Boru's burial place is marked by a distinctive stone slab on the outside wall of the North Transept of the church. It is said that his body lay in state at Armagh for twelve successive nights before being interred in a stone coffin in the Cathedral.

Inside St Patrick's, there is a beautiful stained-glass portrait of Patrick as a young man and, significantly,

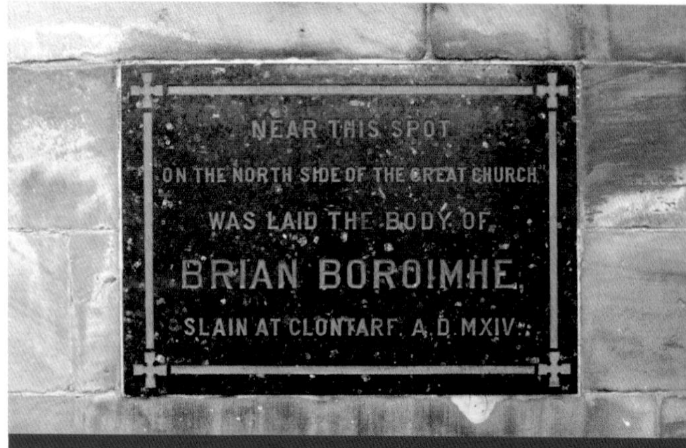

Memorial to Brian Boru at St Patrick's Church of Ireland Cathedral, Armagh

he is dressed in a toga – thus underlining his status as a citizen of Roman Britain. There is, however, a more traditional portrait of Patrick in a stained-glass window behind the altar, depicting him as a still young but more Biblical figure laying the foundation stone of his first main church in 445 AD.

The Cathedral itself is neat and compact, and just inside the entrance is a distinctive tablet with the names of all the Abbots, Bishops and Archbishops from Patrick's era until the present time. A stone church of varying kinds has been situated on this site for over 1,500 years, but during the troubled centuries of Irish history, the

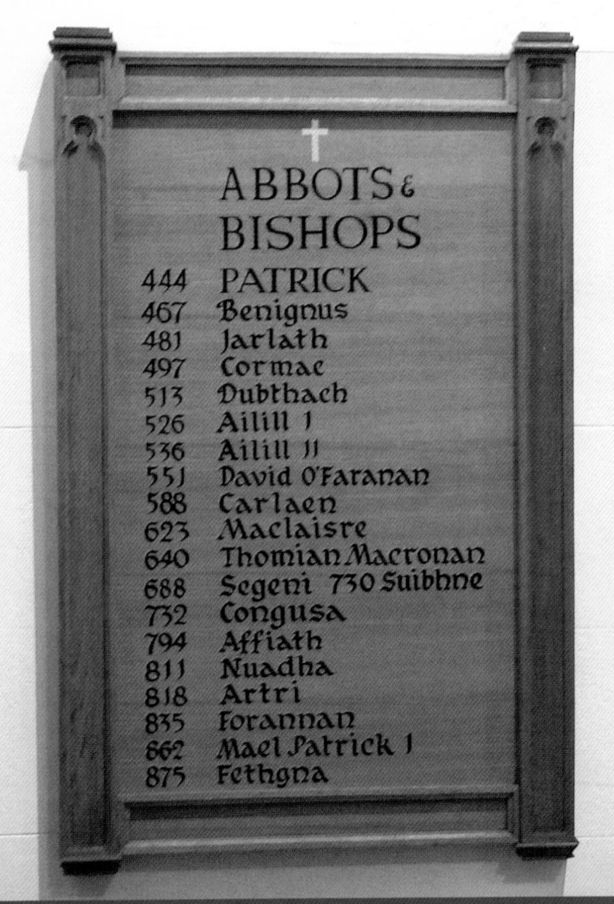

ABBOTS &
BISHOPS
444 PATRICK
467 Benignus
481 Jarlath
497 Cormac
513 Dubthach
526 Ailill I
536 Ailill II
551 David O'Faranan
588 Carlaen
623 Maclaisre
640 Thomian Macronan
688 Segeni 730 Suibhne
732 Congusa
794 Affiath
811 Nuadha
818 Artri
835 Forannan
862 Mael Patrick I
875 Fethgna

Tablet at St Patrick's Church of Ireland Cathedral showing Patrick as Ireland's first Bishop

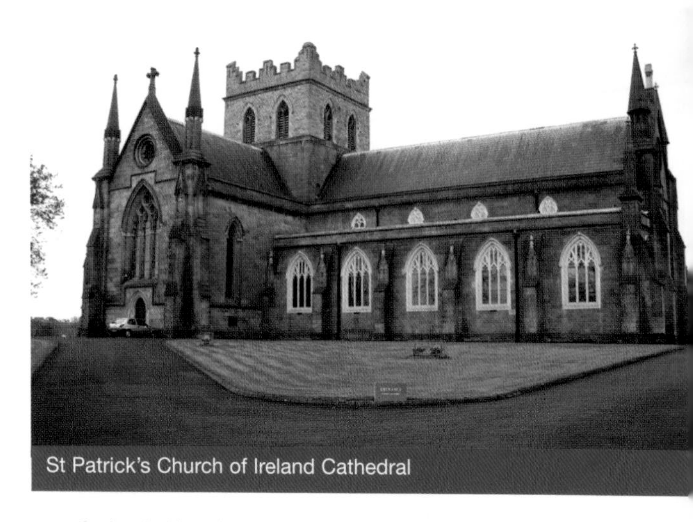
St Patrick's Church of Ireland Cathedral

Cathedral has been rebuilt on at least 17 occasions – and quite recently it has been beautifully restored. The writer William Thackeray visited the Cathedral in the 1840s and described it as "neat and trim like a lady's drawing-room. It wants a hundred years at least to cool the raw colour of the stones, and to dull the brightness of the gilding." This has taken place, to good effect.

The equally impressive Roman Catholic Cathedral stands on a site historically known as Sandy Hill (in the Gaelic *Tealach na Licci*) where Patrick is said to have rescued a young deer. Apparently the local chieftain Daire granted him land on the hill where a fawn and a doe were lying.

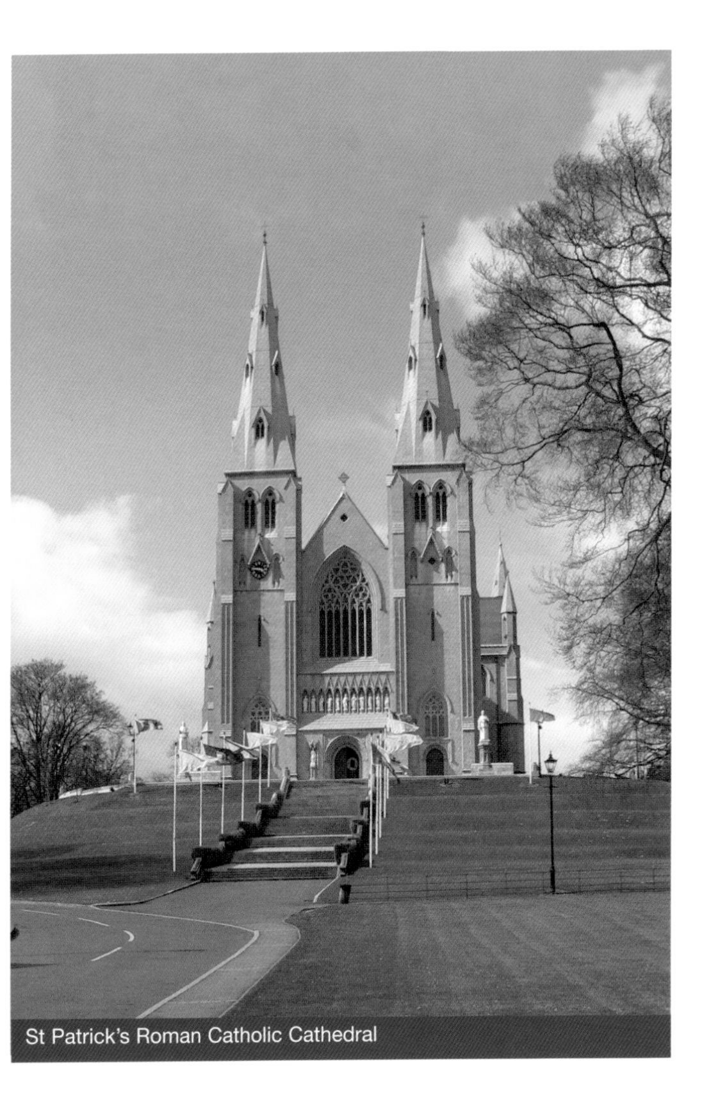

St Patrick's Roman Catholic Cathedral

Patrick's followers wanted to kill the fawn, but the Saint forbade them to do so, and he carried the vulnerable animal on his shoulders to "a safe place", with its young doe following. This "safe place" is traditionally the hill on which the Cathedral is built, and thus maintains a direct link with St Patrick.

This Roman Catholic Cathedral looks directly across a valley of buildings to its Protestant counterpart. Both churches stand like twin pillars of Christendom with distinct historical backgrounds, yet with an allegiance to the same God. In this Cathedral there is, notably, an historic portrayal in one of the stained-glass windows which was installed long before the word 'ecumenical' had been invented. This is a magnificent portrait of St Patrick, attired as a Bishop with a large Cross in his left hand, as he baptises two Irish Princesses at the Fountain of Clebach. High above this charming picture are the portrayals of the Protestant and Roman Catholic Cathedrals, each in a hearted-shaped window. This vision of the common roots of Christianity is not just symbolic – in recent decades the Archbishops of Armagh from both traditions have worked together closely for peace and reconciliation in a divided community.

Interior of St Patrick's Roman Catholic Cathedral

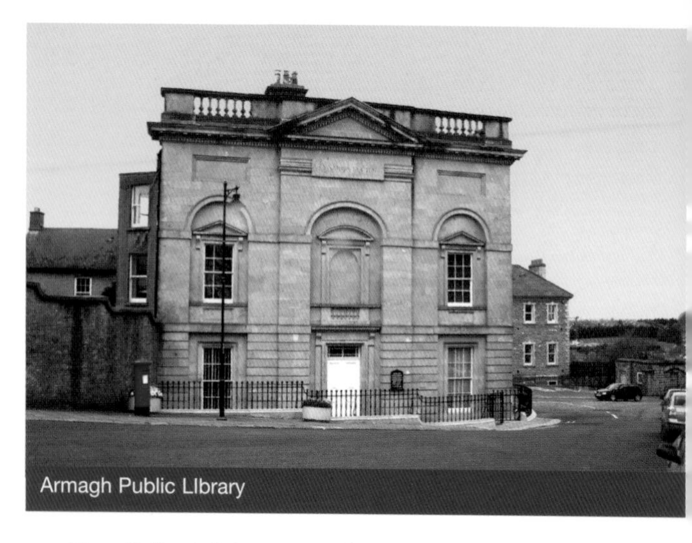
Armagh Public LIbrary

The Cathedral has several other windows depicting St Patrick supposedly receiving his mission from Pope Celestine, his baptism of Daire, his dream and also his death. The magnificent architecture of the building itself adds to the beauty of the artwork. The construction was begun on St Patrick's Day 1840, but the work was suspended seven years later during the Great Irish Famine, and the money was used to help feed the people.

Construction recommenced later on, but a 'Famine Line' showing the break in building is still a feature of the Cathedral. It was completed in 1904, and recently refurbished extensively as one of the most beautiful churches in Ireland.

Each Cathedral is well worth a visit, and they tell their individual and collective stories of the influence of Christianity on the development of the island and its peoples. They are within walking distance of one another, but there is also adequate parking at each. Visitors might like to consider spending between two and three hours, at least, for a combined visit.

Though the Cathedrals are impressive and distinctive in their own right, there is much else to see in Armagh. Near the centre, and just down the hill from the Church of Ireland Cathedral, is St Patrick's Trian, a first-rate exhibition centre which places St Patrick and Armagh in historical perspective. Incidentally, the Trian Centre derives its name from the division of the ancient city into three districts or 'trians'.

This attractive and visually imaginative complex has several main exhibition themes, including the story of Armagh from ancient times, to St Patrick and beyond – as well as the "Land of Lilliput". This features the famous book *Gulliver's Travels* written by Jonathan Swift, who as a young clergyman had connections with the Armagh area. The Trian complex also has a good restaurant, a tourist information centre and gift shops.

For those visitors who have time for more detailed research, the Armagh Public Library, dating from 1771, is situated on the hill just below the Church of Ireland Cathedral. This has been recently refurbished in style, and contains much material from the library of a former Church of Ireland Archbishop Richard Robinson, an 18th-century benefactor who did much to bestow on Armagh its Georgian splendour. The former Archbishop's Palace, at the Demesne some little distance away, is now the headquarters of the local council. In this area there is also the attractive Palace Stables living history exhibition which gives a vivid picture of the life in Armagh in Georgian times. At the entrance to the Demesne there are also the remains of a splendid Franciscan Friary, dating from the mid-13th century, and the longest in Ireland.

Across on the other Armagh hill, just behind the Roman Catholic St Patrick's Cathedral, is the O'Fiaich Memorial Library and Archive. This contains important historical material with an essentially Irish theme, including the Gaelic language. Visitors can also hear songs and poems from South Armagh here.

The Library and Archive is named after the late Cardinal Tomas O'Fiaich, who was Archbishop of Armagh and Roman Catholic Primate from 1977-90. He was a native of South Armagh, and had a notable academic career before his elevation to the Primacy. He was a noted historian, but was also a warm-hearted and popular prelate who could relate to all kinds of people. The Centre has an exhibition on Cardinal O'Fiaich's life and times and areas of interest including local history, music and culture.

Cardinal O'Fiaich's tomb, with those of former Archbishops Conway and D'Alton, is situated in a neatly maintained and accessible plot on the right-hand side of the hill, just below the Cathedral.

The city's historical background is also featured in the Armagh County Museum, on the resplendent Georgian Mall. This has a large collection of materials and artefacts which provide a comprehensive history of Armagh and its origins. Incidentally, although Armagh is technically a 'city' (due to its cathedral), it is the size of a small town – even by Irish standards – and all of the historic sites are easily accessible within a short driving distance and, for the exercise-conscious, even on foot.

Navan Fort

The exception to this is the Navan Fort and Visitor Centre, several miles from the centre of Armagh. Navan was the seat of the Ulster Kings, and the capital of the Province of Ulster from roughly 660 BC until 330 AD. Navan Fort, also known as *Emain Macha*, was a significant place in the early history of Ulster and it was natural that the canny St Patrick would wish to locate his first main church near such a centre of political power. The Navan Fort and Visitor Centre provides valuable material which places the development of Armagh in its important early context.

Armagh as an historic and ecclesiastical centre lies at the heart of the spirit of St Patrick, whose thoughts from his

Navan Centre

autobiographical *Confessio* resonate down through the ages to the Primatial city of today;

"I pray those who believe and fear God, whosoever deigns to look at or receive this writing which Patrick, a sinner, unlearned, has composed in Ireland, that no one should ever say that it was my ignorance, if I did or showed forth anything however small according to God's good pleasure; but let this be your conclusion and let it so be thought, that – as is the perfect truth – it was the gift of God. This is my confession before I die."

Armagh is an essential stopping place in the journey of those who want find out more about the story of Ireland and its Patron Saint.

LOCATIONS

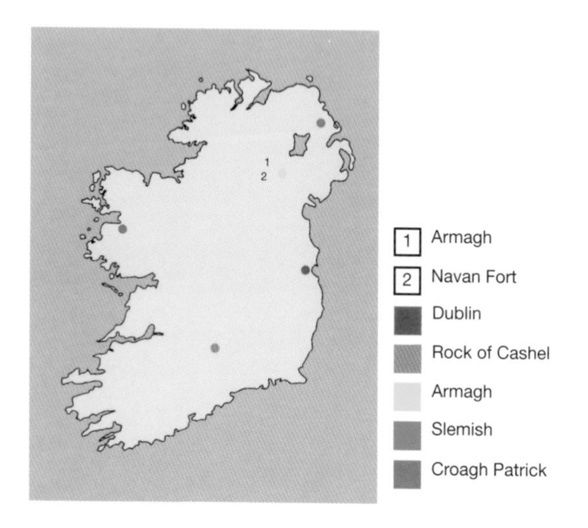

DIRECTIONS

The city is well worth at least a half-day visit and preferably longer. The traffic can be busy in the narrow streets away from The Mall, but there is good parking at St Patrick's Trian Centre, as a base for the inner city, and also at the two Cathedrals and the Bishop's Palace in the Demesne.

Armagh is easily accessible from Belfast on the M1 motorway, turning off at the Portadown junction and taking the A3. From Newry it is accessible via the A28, passing Markethill. Another slightly longer route geographically but perhaps faster in terms of traffic is to stay on the M1 motorway until near Dungannon and then take the A29, through the village of Moy.

St Patrick's Grave outside Down Cathedral

The Heart of Down

The symbolic heart of St Patrick lies under a large gravestone outside the stately Church of Ireland Cathedral in Downpatrick. The large block of Mourne granite, from Ballymagreghan near Castlewellan, is said to mark Patrick's final resting place – though as with so much else in the Saint's life the historical details are sketchy.

Some sources claim that Patrick first landed on the Irish coast at Wicklow and made his way north to the area of Carlingford Lough and eventually landed at the Slaney River (known in Gaelic as *Inbher Slane*) near present-day Saul, a few miles from Downpatrick. Tradition suggests that a local ruler called Dichu was one of Patrick's first converts and he gave the Saint a rudimentary stable or barn in which to shelter from the inclement Irish weather. The Irish term for stable is *Sabhal*, and the English derivation became Saul. To underline the connection, there is a huge grey statue of the Saint on top of a hill near Saul called Slieve Patrick – though access is not easy for those with walking difficulties.

According to legend, Patrick decided around this time to visit his old slave-master Miliucc in the north at Slemish, near Ballymena, as a Christian gesture of reconciliation. However it is said that the wretched Miliucc feared that Patrick would put an evil spell on him, so he built a funeral pyre and burnt himself to death. Such stories can neither be proved nor disproved, but they are all part of the colourful Patrician tradition, which also suggests that Patrick died in the Saul area.

However there is no doubt that Saul itself is an ancient ecclesiastical site. An abbey stood here in the medieval period, and was restored by St Malachy – a friend of St Bernard of Clairvaux – in the mid-12th century. In 1306 it was described as "the church of Saul with the chapel of Ballyculter". Two stone buildings nearby date from the medieval period.

The origin of the present Church of Ireland structure dates from 1788, and a description published in 1830 notes that "the outside is of the plainest architecture, the interior is neat and comfortable. There is not any gallery." This building was later demolished to make way for the current church which was built to mark the putative 1,500th anniversary of St Patrick's arrival in Ireland as a missionary.

St Patrick's statue at summit of Slieve Patrick

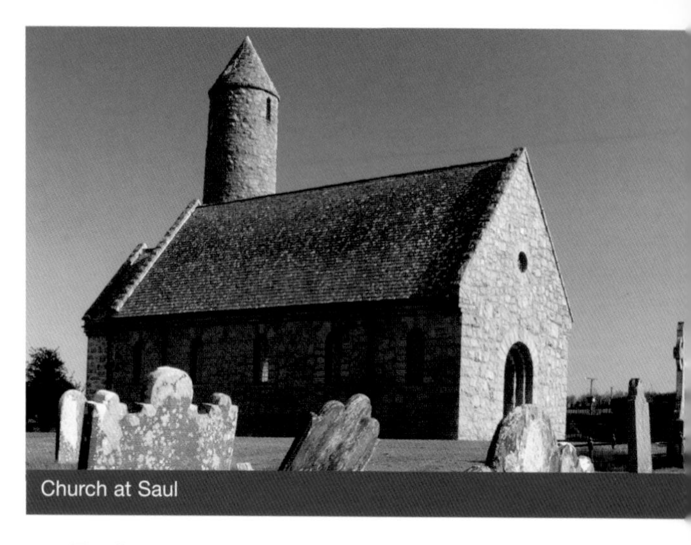
Church at Saul

The foundation stone was laid on Ascension Day in 1933, and the church was consecrated on 1 November in the same year. It remains an attractive building – much more photogenic than its predecessor – and there is much here to interest the visitor. In an adjoining burial-ground, a number of ancient headstones tell their own fascinating story.

Each year on St Patrick's Day there is a service of Holy Communion at Saul, and this is followed by a procession of clergy and the faithful to Downpatrick for a cross-community service in the Cathedral. Afterwards, a wreath is laid on Patrick's grave. The earlier procession roughly follows the route taken by the white oxen who were

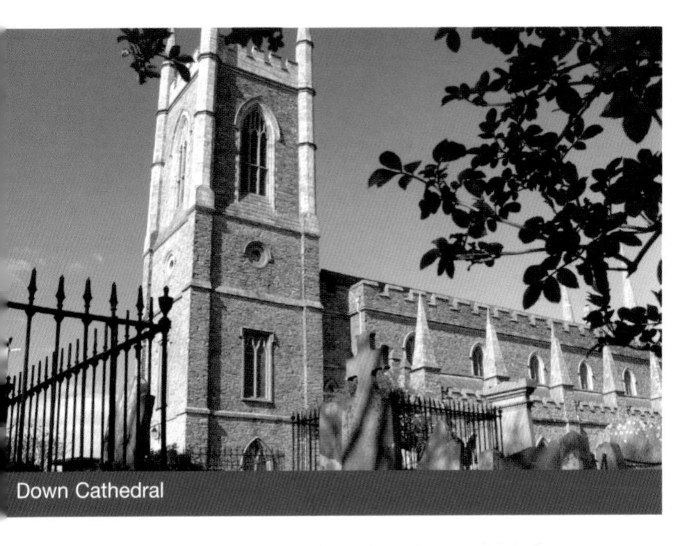

Down Cathedral

believed to have stopped at the place which became the site of Patrick's grave just outside the Cathedral. The grave itself is plain, but impressive. The heart-shaped granite stone bears a simple cross, with the lettering "Patric". This stone was put in place in 1902 by Francis Joseph Bigger and his friends from the Belfast Naturalists' Field Club. Before that time, people visiting the supposed grave would scoop up some earth and bring it away with them as a souvenir of their visit. This led gradually to the formation of an undignified dip in the ground – hence the placing of the granite stone to prevent the total erosion of the site. Perhaps this was an early-20th century example of good conservation practice.

A much more likely story is that this spot was chosen by the 12th-century Norman overlord John de Courcy who had ousted the local ruler. He wished to ingratiate himself with the people of the area, and – almost miraculously – he 'discovered' the ancient bones of St Patrick. He even persuaded Pope Urban III to send Cardinal Vivian from Rome to represent him at the re-burial of Patrick's remains. Accordingly a strong tradition developed about Patrick's burial-place at Downpatrick. As noted earlier, historians are uncertain whether or not Patrick is actually buried here, though happily this does not seem to diminish its sanctity for visitors and locals alike.

There is, however, a much surer historical foundation for the establishment of Down Cathedral on the site of an ancient monastery mentioned in the Irish Annals. The site, not surprisingly, was taken over by the aforementioned John de Courcy who astutely calculated the value of establishing a new church on an ancient site right beside the supposed burial-place of St Patrick himself. De Courcy established a Benedictine Abbey, named after the Saint, and it survived various setbacks and calamities – including a rare Irish earthquake in 1245. Unfortunately it was unable to survive the dissolution of the monasteries in 1541.

For the next 250 years, the former monastery lay in virtual ruins although its walls remained in place. Then in 1790 the public-spirited first Marquis of Downshire and the Church of Ireland Dean of Down, the Honourable and Reverend William Annesley, began a restoration of the building which was destined to become the Cathedral Church of the Diocese. It was completed and consecrated in 1818, though the tower was not finished until 1829.

The modern structure is substantially that of the earlier Cathedral, with relatively minor alterations down the decades. The pews are original, and in the mid-1980s the Cathedral was closed for two years to complete an exact replica of the interior of the 19th-century building. The Cathedral also has a fine organ case, and an organ was donated by King George III early in the 19th century. It is said that John Wesley, the founder of Methodism who visited Ireland several times, was banned from preaching in Anglican pulpits. However, with typical ingenuity he preached persuasively in the open air, just outside the Cathedral.

Today Down Cathedral is a focal point for important ecclesiastical and cross-community civic events. It is a place not only to visit, but which also offers an

St Patrick Centre, Downpatrick

atmosphere away from the busy world where the visitor can reflect upon St Patrick's immense contribution to Irish Christianity which later on had profound implications on the European continent.

Those appreciative of a modern presentation of this important story, complete with technological wizardry, should visit Downpatrick's excellent St Patrick Centre which offers a comprehensive account of the life and times of Ireland's Patron Saint. There is a spectacular cinema-style overview, and several interactive exhibitions which are particularly attractive to young people. The Centre also contains a library as well as other important historical data, an art gallery, a craft shop and a Tourist Information Centre. There is also a cafe, which allows the visitor to pause at this important Centre, which should not be missed by anyone with an interest in St Patrick.

For those who would like to browse through the more detailed history of the area, the nearby Down County Museum on English Street has a wealth of fascinating material. The building was formerly an 18th-century gaol where Thomas Russell, a United Irishman, was hanged for alleged conspiracy against the Crown. A memorial stone to Russell was placed in the local parish church

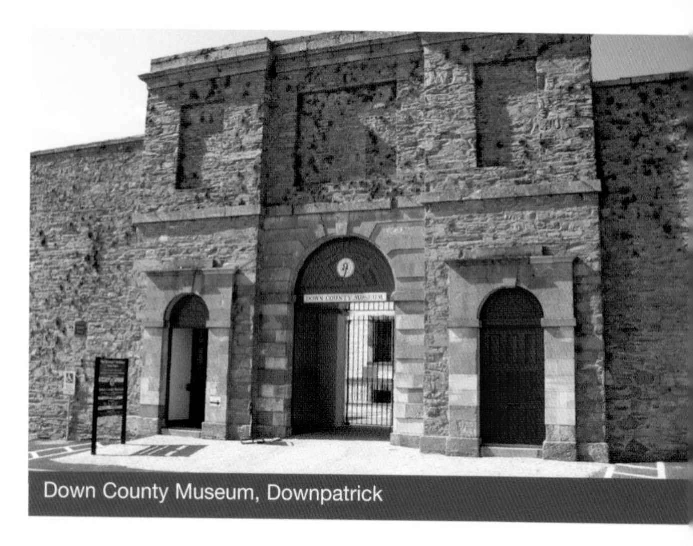

Down County Museum, Downpatrick

graveyard by Mary Anne McCracken, the sister of yet another leading Irish Republican Henry Joy McCracken. He was hanged at Cornmarket in Belfast for taking part in the 1798 Rebellion.

The County Museum also has an authentically-restored Governor's House, and also the gaol cells which detained local prisoners prior to their deportation to distant colonies – where, ironically, many of them flourished. Nevertheless, the reality of such stern measures and the reports of revolution and counter-revolution might well have had the Christian and peace-loving St Patrick turning in his Downpatrick grave.

Struell Wells

Inch Abbey near Downpatrick

There are other Patrician connections in the wider area, and in the Lecale region east of Bishopscourt about a mile from Saul and two miles from Downpatrick are the Struell Wells, which retain a reputation for miraculous healing, dating back to the earliest times. A number of similar 'Holy Wells' are situated in many parts of Ireland, but according to legend it was St Patrick himself who blessed the Struell Wells, thus giving them healing properties. Some scholars believe, however, that these existed from ancient times and that the early Christian Church was adept at adopting and adapting such pre-Christian practices for its own outreach. There are four Struell Wells, two of them roofed, and the pilgrimage tradition continues even in the era of modern medicine.

The remains of the 12th-century Inch Abbey, accessible and sign-posted from the main Downpatrick to Belfast Road, are redolent of John de Courcy and St Patrick whose paths crossed – in a manner of speaking – at the gravesite outside Down Cathedral. The bold de Courcy, intent on extending Norman influence, destroyed a nearby Cistercian Abbey in a warlike mode. Later, however, he made amends by building a new monastery at Inch and inviting some Lancashire-based Cistercians to occupy it – thus subtly extending English influence in the Province of Ulster. John de Courcy, however, was always mindful of maintaining as good relations as possible with the local populace, and – not surprisingly – he commissioned a Cistercian monk named Jocelin to write a history of St Patrick. This was, no doubt, the first of many hagiographies about Patrick which freely blended fact and fiction. Inch Abbey, however, retains the solid stones of history which tell their own story.

Another link with St Patrick is the former Nendrum Monastery on Mahee Island at Strangford Lough. This is accessible from Downpatrick on the A22 through Balloo and Killinchy. The attractive Nendrum site, surrounded by water on three sides, has the remains of the monastery established

Nendrum Monastery, Mahee Island, Co. Down

by St Machaoi. He was said to be a contemporary of St Patrick, and the monastery was reputed to have provided a wealth of local converts who in turn formed Christian communities in other parts of Ireland, the British Isles and further afield. Between the 6th and 8th centuries this Irish 'flowering' was indeed impressive – with establishments in Lindisfarne, Liege, Cologne, Wurzburg, Salzburg, Vienna, Lucca, and many other places.

At Nendrum there is an interpretive centre which helps to set the local history in context. There is also information on Greyabbey, situated across the Lough and accessible through the town of Newtownards, at some little distance

Grey Abbey, Ards Peninsula

away. Greyabbey was founded in the late-12th century by none other than Affreca, the wife of John de Courcy, and a contemporary display gives a glimpse of the monastic life in the Ireland of the time. It also underlines the extent of influence of Norman rule in the North of Ireland.

Thus the story of the ancient Irish, the foreign missionaries such as Patrick, and the Norman invaders including John de Courcy, is inextricably linked in the beautiful and historic countryside at the heart of Down. The visitor who has time to spend in this area will learn much about St Patrick and also discover many of the elements which have fused to produce the Ireland, north and south, of modern times.

LOCATIONS

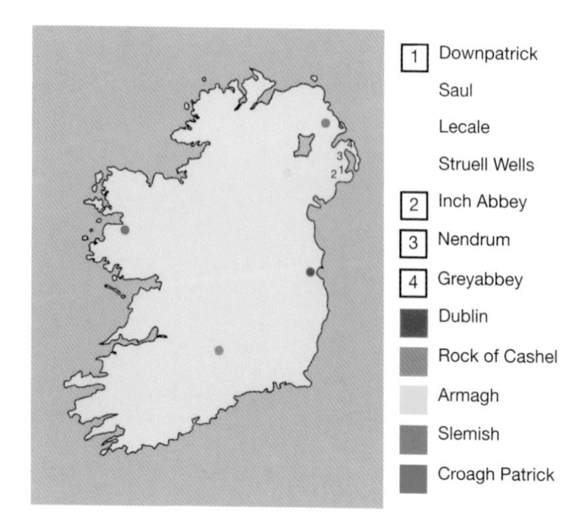

DIRECTIONS

A one-day visit from Belfast, with an early start, should be sufficient to cover the trail of St Patrick and surrounding countryside – leaving time for lunch and also for dinner, perhaps on the way back. A suggested itinerary, travelling anti-clockwise, is to leave Belfast and travel south-east on the A24 to Carryduff, and then along the A7 (the same route) through Saintfield and Crossgar, and on to Downpatrick which provides the main focus of the visit. The return journey, with a diversion to Struell Wells, can be made back via Inch Abbey, and then on the A22, with another diversion to Nendrum, and back through Comber to east Belfast. However, those who wish to visit Greyabbey can travel to Comber and then to Newtownards on the A21. From there the A20 leads to Greyabbey. Depending on the time spent at Greyabbey this diversion will add possibly more than an hour to the overall itinerary.

Slemish

Slemish, County Antrim

Slemish near Ballymena in Co. Antrim, is a medium-sized mountain of volcanic origin where St Patrick is thought to have spent six years of his youth. He was taken there as a slave, and had to herd animals for his master, reputedly named Miliucc. He mentions being taken captive and working as a slave in his autobiographical *Confessio* though as with much else concerning his life, he was not precise about the location of the place.

He refers to the geographical area of his captivity as "Silva Focluti", and some scholars surmise that this might have been anywhere from Co. Mayo in the West of Ireland to Magherafelt, Strangford Lough and Faughal, near Cushendall in the North. Nevertheless, Slemish mountain is traditionally regarded as Patrick's place of servitude, and each year there is a pilgrimage to the 180 metre summit on St Patrick's Day, 17 March.

It is clear, however, that Patrick believed that the period of captivity was a significant and formative part of his early life, which led to his Christian conversion and ultimately to his mission in Ireland. He writes about this period movingly and graphically in his *Confessio*, when he declares that "about the age of sixteen" he was taken captive to Ireland.

"BUT AFTER I CAME TO IRELAND – EVERY DAY I HAD TO TEND

SHEEP, AND MANY TIMES A DAY I PRAYED –

THE LOVE OF GOD AND HIS FEAR CAME TO ME MORE AND MOR

AND MY FAITH WAS STRENGTHENED."

"I did not know the true God. I was taken into captivity to Ireland with many thousands of people – and deservedly so, because we turned away from God, and did not keep His commandments, and did not obey our priests, who used to remind us of our salvation." In his captivity, however, he had a remarkable spiritual re-awakening. He writes:

"But after I came to Ireland – every day I had to tend sheep, and many times a day I prayed – the love of God and His fear came to me more and more, and my faith was strengthened. And my spirit was moved so that in a single day I would say as many as a hundred prayers, and almost as many in the night, and this even when I was staying in the woods, and on the mountains: and I used to get up for prayer before daylight, through snow, through frost, through rain, and I felt no harm, and there was no sloth in me – as I now see, because the spirit within me was then fervent." He then goes on to explain how he heard a voice in his dream telling him that he would escape, which he eventually did.

This tough yet ultimately creative experience of Patrick in captivity is easy to visualise amid the rugged beauty of Slemish, in a broad area where the people of both main religious traditions have traditionally been spiritually aware, resourceful and self-reliant. It is also one of the oldest-inhabited parts of Ireland, with a story going back to pre-history. The area where Patrick is thought to have tended the animals for his master Miliucc on Slemish is generally known as 'the Swine Craes'.

Slemish is best reached by road through the attractive village of Broughshane, several miles away. The circular climb to the summit of the mountain is steep and rocky in parts, and can be difficult in wet weather, when visitors should take particular care. The weather unfortunately can be changeable, and the locals say that they can sometimes experience all four seasons of the year in the space of a single day.

Those who wish to climb Slemish are advised to use the marked route, and to equip themselves with stout footwear and all-weather protective clothing – and perhaps also carry a walking-stick. Dogs must be kept on a lead at all times. The climb, however, is worthwhile and on a good day the visitor can obtain excellent views of the surrounding Braid Valley, the Sperrins, Lough Neagh – the largest inland lake in the British Isles – and even Scotland.

Around Slemish there is an attractive range of wildlife, and bird-watchers might be fortunate enough to spot

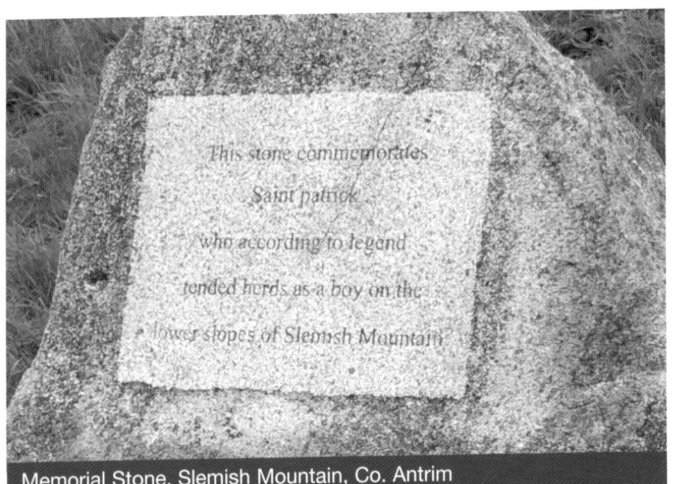

Memorial Stone, Slemish Mountain, Co. Antrim

buzzards with their characteristic markings, or more likely a family of black ravens which are familiar in the area. The meadow pipit and – in spring – the wheatear, are not uncommon.

There is an interpretive display on the life of St Patrick at the start of the walk, and also toilets. However there are no catering facilities available at present. The round trip of approximately 1.5 km should take at least an hour in good weather, and there is no sense of time pressure in a place where Patrick may have had all the time in the world to search his soul and to find his path back to God.

St Patrick's Church, Broughshane, Co. Antrim

As well as Slemish there is much else to see in the area, including the award-winning Broughshane which is ablaze with flowers in season and is known as 'the Garden Village of Ulster.' There are also good local cafes and restaurants.

The village has a St Patrick's Church of Ireland, and there is also a St Patrick's in Ballymena – the bustling centre of the region. On the other side of the town is the beautiful village of Gracehill, which developed from a centuries-old Moravian settlement. The distinctive church and housing in the village retain a special period flavour, and the Moravian cemetery still maintains the custom of separating the graves of its former male and female members.

LOCATIONS

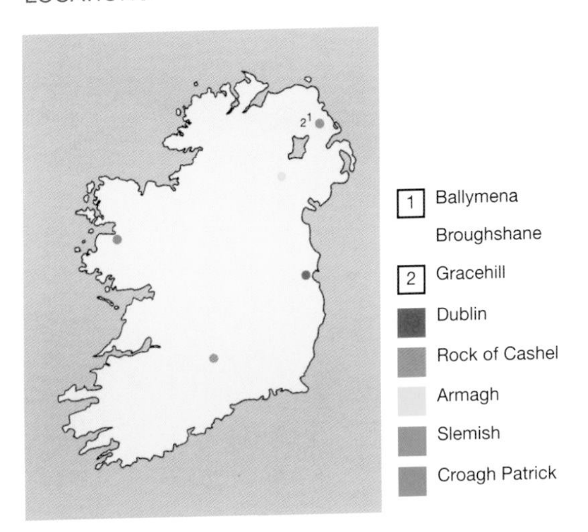

DIRECTIONS

Slemish is best accessed via the M2 motorway from Belfast, branching off at the junction leading to Broughshane, and from thence to the base of the mountain. The other areas mentioned including Ballymena and Gracehill are also well signposted.

Statue of 'Patrick the Pilgrim' at Lough Derg

Lough Derg and Carndonagh Pilgrimage

Lough Derg, some four miles from the village of Pettigo in south Donegal, is the focus of a long-established and traditional pilgrimage associated with 'St Patrick's Purgatory.'

According to legend, Patrick spent 40 days in prayer and fasting on Station Island amid this rugged and beautiful landscape. There are various interpretations of Patrick's links with the island. Some sources claim that Lough Derg, sometimes known as 'the red lake', was derivative of the blood drawn by the Saint when he slew a huge serpent there. In this version there are echoes of the famous legend of Patrick banishing the snakes, or serpents, from Ireland.

Others believe that Lough Derg refers to "the lake of the cave" and to the place where Patrick had a final showdown with the ancient druids. In yet another legend, Lough Derg is the place – where in a deep cave – Patrick saw a vision of Purgatory. Historically this was given a certain authenticity by the existence of a former cave or deep hollow on Station Island. This drew pilgrims to 'St Patrick's Cave' until the end of the 18th century and it later became the site of

ST PATRICK AND 'THE SNAKES'

St Patrick is reputed to have driven 'the snakes' from Ireland. The trouble is that Ireland is not known for its snakes as such. How, therefore, could this supposed connection have arisen?

Two Irish writers Father John Walsh and Thomas Bradley offer an ingenious explanation in their book *A History of the Irish Church 400-700 AD* published by the Columba Press. Large sections of the Irish society of Patrick's era were notably promiscuous, with trial marriages, multiple partners, and various sexual relationships. One of the symbols of the horned god worshipped by the pagans was that of a serpent, widely regarded as a phallic symbol.

Walsh and Bradley surmise that "It is probably no coincidence that the medieval carving of St Patrick from Faughart, Co. Louth, now in the National Museum of Ireland, has the saint trampling on a serpent. Patrick's supposed banishment of all the serpents from Ireland may be a vivid and subtle way of recalling how he destroyed pagan devotion to the horned god and its attendant serpents."

In other words Patrick did not so much banish the 'snakes' from Ireland, as symbolically stamp on the serpent of sensuality which characterised the Ireland of his day. What, one wonders, would he make of the Ireland of today?

Departure Point for Station Island, Lough Derg

a church. At one stage a second cave was open on the nearby 'Saint's Island' but this was closed by an order from the Vatican in the late 15th century.

Incidentally, in Roman Catholic teaching the term 'Purgatory' received prominence as a state of a continuing process of purification after death, and the association between Station Island as a place of 'St Patrick's Purgatory' has remained for centuries in the consciousness of countless pilgrims from Ireland and overseas. It is believed that Patrick left a disciple named Davog, a Welshman, in the area which is generally known in the Irish as *Termon Davog*, literally Davog's church-lands.

According to records, St Patrick's Purgatory was prominent on maps of medieval Ireland, and particularly between the 12-15th centuries, many famous pilgrims from mainland Europe came to Lough Derg – though the vast majority came from Ireland. These are said to have included the famous Irish harpist and composer Turlough O'Carolan, whose likeness is preserved in St Patrick's Cathedral in Dublin – not far from a modern statue of St Patrick himself by the sculptress Melanie Le Brocquy.

Like much else in Ireland, the pilgrimages to Lough Derg were subject to the vicissitudes of history – including suppression by the state authorities, and it is said that when pilgrims were unable to cross to Station Island itself, they remained on the edge of the shore to fast and pray there. There was a marked drop in the number of pilgrims after the Great Famine of the mid-19th century, and between 1870-1900 the yearly number of pilgrims averaged only about 3,000. However there was a significant increase since the beginning of the 20th century, and currently there are around 30,000 a year.

The boat shown here was used to ferry pilgrims to Station Island up until 1988. It was named the *St Patrick* and may have replaced an earlier boat of the same name. It was built just 30 metres from its current resting place where the statue of 'Patrick the Pilgrim' currently stands. The boat was licensed to hold 150 people and is reputed to have been the largest rowing boat in Ireland. Twelve men were needed to row it and it was rowed by hand until the early 1960s when it was towed by a motorised boat named *St Brigid.*

There are Three-Day pilgrimages each year between 1 June and 15 August inclusive. These are not for the faint-hearted, but those who participate will testify to the well-being experienced from this period of intensive prayer, penance and inner peace. Pilgrims must be at least 15 years old, in normal good health and able to walk and kneel without help. They are required to undertake a fast from the midnight prior to their arrival, and they are asked to bring warm and waterproof clothing. Access to the island is by boat, and these are available from 11am until 3pm each day. The only serious accident on the history of the Pilgrimage was in 1795 when some 90 people perished in relatively shallow water just off Friar's Island. The boat began to take in water and in the ensuing panic it capsized with the huge loss of life.

Pilgrims are asked to arrive at Station Island between 11am-3pm on the first day, during which three 'Stations' or prayers are made at the so-called 'Penitential Beds', which are the remains of former beehive monastic cells near the church named St Mary of the Angels, dating from 1870 and on the site of a former Franciscan church of the same name. On the site of the former Pilgrims' Cave is the Basilica. This impressive octagonal building which was consecrated in 1931 can seat up to 1150 people, and is one of focal points of the modern pilgrimages. For those who have an eye for art, the Basilica contains beautiful stained-glass windows by Harry Clarke.

Throughout their three-day visit the pilgrims go barefoot and recite some 280 prayers at each of nine stations. They do not sleep on the first night, but are able to stay in hostel accommodation on the island during the second night.

They are allowed one meal a day, which consists of dry bread or oatcakes, and they can drink black tea or coffee. There are strict rules, including the prohibition of food (other than the above-mentioned), as well as sweets, chewing-gum, alcoholic and other drinks.

To maintain a reflective silence in an age where humans are subjected to a daily cacophony of sound, mobile phones are prohibited, as are radios and personal stereos, musical instruments or games. Pilgrims are not allowed to use cameras, or to sell or distribute articles and literature. No reservations are required for the Three-Day Pilgrimage, during which the spiritual exercises and physical penance have changed little since the 17th century.

Lough Derg also offers One-Day Retreats on specific dates from May until September, in an atmosphere for reflection and renewal. These are not suitable for children, but they are open to all adults – and particularly those who are unable to take part in the Three-Day Pilgrimage.

The One-Day Retreats do not require fasting or walking bare-footed, but numbers are limited, and advance booking is essential. Individual retreats for individuals or couples can be arranged with the Prior, outside the traditional Three Day Pilgrimage. There are also a small number of Quiet Days, but numbers are limited, and prior consultation is advisable.

The Lough Derg pilgrimages have retained the essence of reflection and spirituality in the midst of a busy world. The Prior Msgr Richard Mohan sums it up thus; "In earlier times the area around the lake was a place of protection for anyone in trouble. Today Lough Derg is still a safe place, reaching out to all in need, offering reconciliation, healing and peace. Whatever their creed, background, social circumstance or religious practice, all are made welcome."

CARNDONAGH

Carndonagh is an attractive small town near the north-west coast of Donegal's rugged and beautiful Inishowen peninsula. It is believed that St Patrick founded a church, for the brother of the Bishop of Clogher, on the hill where the present Church of Ireland building now stands. This is at the junction of the main road between Buncrana and Ballyliffin.

In the graveyard of the Church is a lintel stone from a previous 12th-century structure. There is also an ancient cross pillar depicting a crucifixion, and a flabellum which, in turn, has an inset resembling a marigold – though scholars are not agreed that it actually is a marigold. Incidentally a flabellum was a liturgical fan which was used to protect the Christian altar from flies and dust. This graveyard, which is still in use, is given a special sense of antiquity by these ancient objects, and by a number of other very old head-stones.

Just outside the Church is a well-preserved St Patrick's Cross, thought to date from around the 7th century. There is a carving of the Christ figure on the east face, and it is regarded as one of the best carved stone crosses in Ireland, as well as one of the most important early Christian relics. It stands some 11.5 feet high, and is flanked by two smaller re-erected pillar stones. One depicts King David as a soldier and also as a musician; the other has a cleric with a crozier and a handbell. All three stones are well-maintained and easily accessible to visitors.

The name of Carndonagh is derived from the Gaelic term *carn domhnach,* literally the 'cairn of domhnach' – a church. Also of interest in Carndonagh is the spectacular Roman Catholic church dating from the mid-20th century and set on a high hill with commanding views over the town.

The St Patrick's Cross is one of the focal points for a visit, but the area is surrounded by attractive countryside and coastlines. On the way to Ballyliffin there is a replica of a 19th-century Famine Village, which is well sign-posted. The area also has good main roads and more than adequate hotels and restaurants. The adventurous might also make their way to Malin Head, which is one of the most northerly points in Ireland.

LOCATIONS

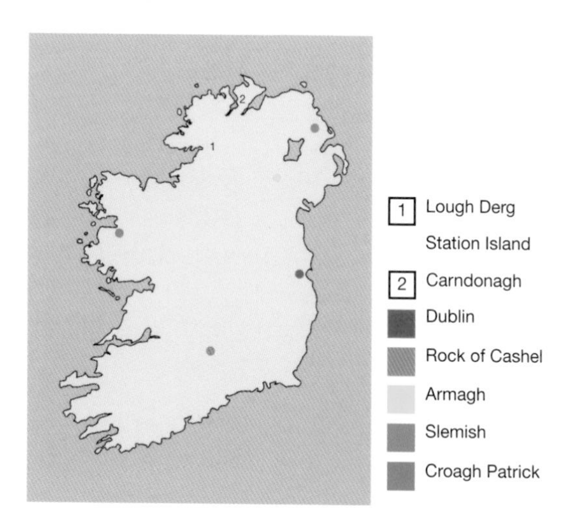

DIRECTIONS

To travel from Larne or Belfast and the north-east, take the M1 motorway and then the A4 road to Ballygawley, branch off to Omagh, Kesh and Pettigo, where Lough Derg is accessible by road. Those travelling from Dublin may take the N3 to Cavan and continue through Enniskillen to Kesh and eventually Pettigo. The route from the West of Ireland at Sligo runs through Bundoran, Ballyshannon, Belleek and Pettigo. Pilgrims are asked to arrive as early as possible on the day of retreat or the first day of the Three Day Pilgrimage. This may require an overnight stay near Lough Derg and there are a number of approved guest houses in the Pettigo area.

Carndonagh is situated on the Inishowen Peninsula, about 18 kms north of Buncrana. Follow the main road (R238) in the direction of Malin Head, Ireland's most northernly point, or change to R244 at Drumfee for a shorter journey.

Croagh Patrick

Croagh Patrick, County Mayo

Croagh Patrick is a rugged and beautiful mountain in the West of Ireland where St Patrick is reputed to have spent forty lonely days and nights in fasting, contemplation and prayer. This tradition has made Croagh Patrick one of the best-known pilgrimage centres in Ireland.

During Patrick's heart-searching back in the 5th century AD, he was said to have been attacked by demons on the mountain which was once the territory of a pagan god called Crom. However, Patrick rang his famous Black Bell – now in the National Irish Museum in Dublin – and the demons departed from the slopes in the form of blackbirds.

It is also said that when Patrick rang his bell loudly at the edge of a precipice on the mountain, all the snakes and toads in Ireland leapt to their deaths – apart from the canny natterjack toad which managed to survive. This legend about driving away the snakes remains one of the most widespread and consistent themes of Patrician folklore.

Tradition also recounts that Patrick's experience on Croagh Patrick was so disturbing that when it was all over he wept with relief. It is said that an angel was sent by God to comfort him, and that Patrick asked for a special dispensation for the Irish people. This also forms part of the basis for his claim to be the Patron Saint of Ireland.

This legend of Croagh Patrick is central to the story of Patrick's victory over paganism, and there are obvious Biblical undertones. These include his forty days and nights of trial, just like Christ's temptation in the wilderness, and also the tribulations of Moses and Elias – all of whom triumphed over adversity and the powers of darkness.

Traditionally the triumph of St Patrick has been the focus of a pilgrimage of many thousands of people to Croagh Patrick, which even in pre-history had its own religious connotations. During a relatively recent archaeological excavation an ancient Celtic hill-fort was discovered at the top of the mountain. It is known that Croagh Patrick was a place of considerable importance in the pre-Christian era, even before the arrival of Patrick and other missionaries – including Palladius who has been mentioned earlier.

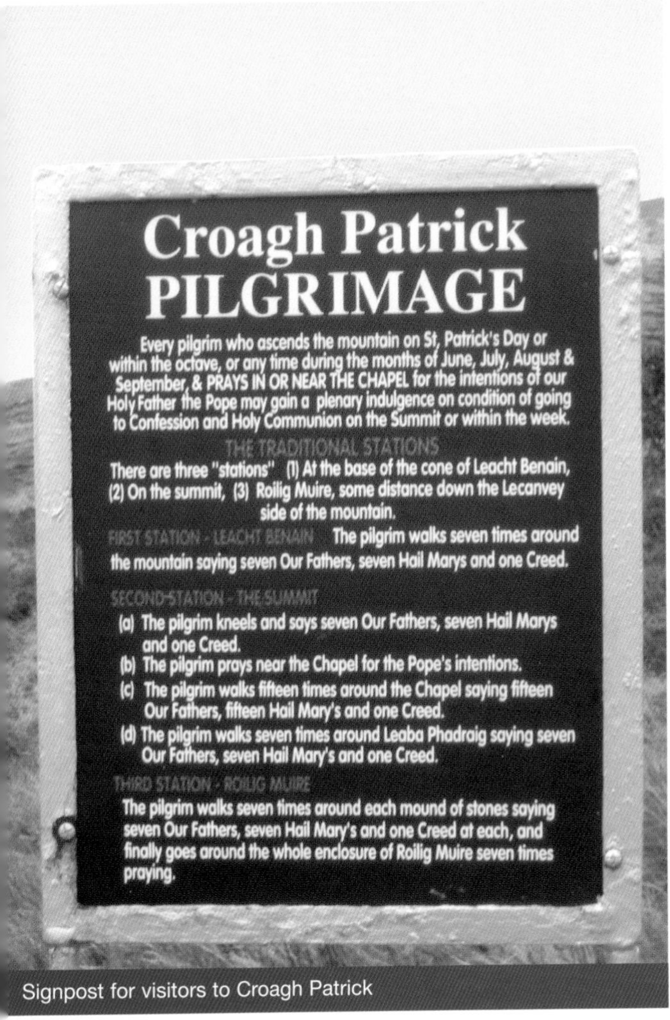

Croagh Patrick
PILGRIMAGE
Every pilgrim who ascends the mountain on St, Patrick's Day or within the octave, or any time during the months of June, July, August & September, & PRAYS IN OR NEAR THE CHAPEL for the intentions of our Holy Father the Pope may gain a plenary indulgence on condition of going to Confession and Holy Communion on the Summit or within the week.
THE TRADITIONAL STATIONS
There are three "stations" (1) At the base of the cone of Leacht Benain, (2) On the summit, (3) Roilig Muire, some distance down the Lecanvey side of the mountain.
FIRST STATION - LEACHT BENAIN The pilgrim walks seven times around the mountain saying seven Our Fathers, seven Hail Marys and one Creed.
SECOND STATION - THE SUMMIT
(a) The pilgrim kneels and says seven Our Fathers, seven Hail Marys and one Creed.
(b) The pilgrim prays near the Chapel for the Pope's intentions.
(c) The pilgrim walks fifteen times around the Chapel saying fifteen Our Fathers, fifteen Hail Mary's and one Creed.
(d) The pilgrim walks seven times around Leaba Phadraig saying seven Our Fathers, seven Hail Mary's and one Creed.
THIRD STATION - ROILIG MUIRE
The pilgrim walks seven times around each mound of stones saying seven Our Fathers, seven Hail Mary's and one Creed at each, and finally goes around the whole enclosure of Roilig Muire seven times praying.

Signpost for visitors to Croagh Patrick

Clew Bay from Croagh Patrick

The tradition of pilgrimage at Croagh Patrick stretches back therefore some 5,000 years, and continues to the present time. Throughout the year people from many backgrounds, and of all ages, ascend the stiff slopes of the mountain as an act of penance and – weather permitting – also to gain magnificent views of Clew Bay and the outstanding Co. Mayo scenery, where Croagh Patrick rises to a height of more than 760 metres above sea level.

However, the main pilgrimage takes place each year on Reek Sunday – the last Sunday in July before the traditional festival of Lughnasa – and up to 30,000 people usually take part. Their motives for doing so are mixed – some regard it as a purifying penance in the place where St Patrick won his important victory over the powers of darkness; for others it is a challenging day out with friends and also a worthwhile achievement in itself. For yet others, the pilgrimage and climb have something of all these elements, and more. Those taking part include religious believers, archaeologists and historians, nature lovers, hill climbers and also enterprising tourists who just want a good story to bring back home.

The climb to the summit, depending on the age, fitness and experience of the climber, takes about two hours, and the descent – surprisingly – can take up to an hour and a half. Climbers are advised to use stout footwear, and all-weather clothing, as the weather in Ireland – particularly in summer – can be unpredictable. It is also advisable to bring drinking liquid, and perhaps a snack, but climbers facing the stiff hike should be careful not to overburden themselves. Climbing-sticks are available for purchase locally.

The main annual pilgrimage starts before dawn at Murrisk Abbey, some 8-9 kms outside Westport, the main town

WHEN CLIMBING
THE MOUNTAIN KEEP
STRICTLY TO THE PATH
DO NOT CLIMB ON WET
OR FOGGY DAYS
Signpost at Croagh Patrick

in the area. In the early darkness, torches are necessary but as the dawn breaks, the light floods symbolically over the mountain and the pilgrims are heartened on their way. The first main stop is at St Patrick's Statue, which for many becomes a place of contemplation and prayer. Although it is not one of the three official stations, or places of prayer, on the pilgrimage, it is a good halting-point for those who do not wish to complete the ascent. Others who press on can celebrate Mass in a tiny chapel at the summit, if they so wish.

Over the years the footsteps of countless people have created a distinctive path which characterises the mountain and can be seen for many miles around. This annual pilgrimage on Reek Sunday is akin to the barefoot penance of the pilgrims to Lough Derg, and many talk later about the religiously purifying experience they have undergone. The climb can be taken, of course, at any time of the year or day, depending on the weather, the availability of the light, and other factors.

A well-equipped Information Centre at Croagh Patrick was opened in 2000, and it is situated in Murrisk on the Pilgrim's Path at the foot of the mountain. It has a restaurant, and it provides information, guided tours,

Pilgrims climbing Croagh Patrick

a craft shop, packed lunches, secure lockers and, for a small fee, the use of showers, which can be yet another blessing after the experience of the climb. Visitors can drive to the car-park of the Information Centre, but the only way to the top of Croagh Patrick – and down again – is on foot.

For visitors wishing to see more of the area, the attractive town of Westport provides a base and there are good tourist facilities. There is also a wide choice of accommodation available, but in high season, advance booking is advisable.

LOCATIONS

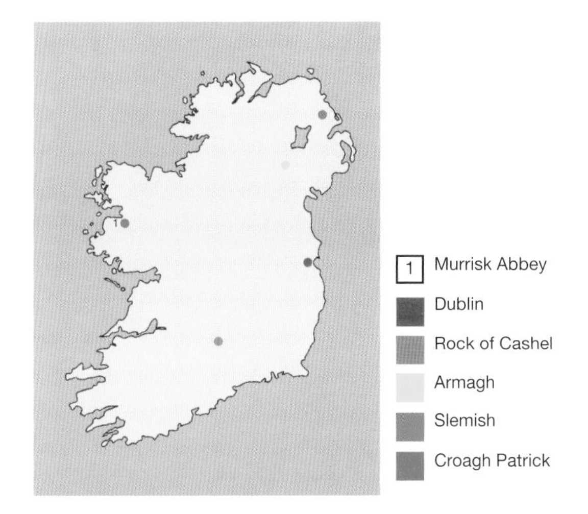

DIRECTIONS

There are good rail and bus services from the main Irish cities like Dublin and Galway to Westport. There is also a small airport at Knock, which provides connection to Dublin, the UK and Europe. Those travelling from the North can do so via Enniskillen and Sligo. The main roads are good and are well sign-posted, though the more difficult roads are those between Enniskillen and Sligo.

Abbey remains at Hill of Slane

Slane and the Hill of Tara

The area around Slane and the Hill of Tara in Co. Meath are associated with one of the legends of vital importance to the success of St Patrick's mission, and it retains a central relevance to the story of Ireland's patron saint.

Tara was the historical seat of the High Kings of Ireland long before the arrival of Christianity, but in this Patrician legend the area was also the scene of a crucial confrontation between the forces of light and darkness from which Patrick emerged triumphant.

The story has different versions, but one of the most dramatic is that recounted by the Irish scribe Muirchu Moccu Machteni, a 7th-century priest in the Armagh archdiocese. He had read an early version of St Patrick's *Confessio*, and wrote a *Life of Patrick* sometime between or about 661 and 700 AD – though he modestly admitted his shortcomings as a biographer. Nevertheless his work became part of the priceless 9th-century manuscript of the *Book of Armagh*.

It was Muirchu who claimed that Patrick first landed on the coast at Wicklow on his missionary journey to Ireland, and later that he had sought a reconciliation with his old

A fine mullioned window in the college at the Franciscan monastery on the Hill of Slane

slave-master Miliucc at Slemish. It was also Muirchu who wrote the vivid story of Patrick's encounter with the pagan King Laoghaire at Tara.

He describes how Patrick and his followers travelled at Easter to the great plain of Brega, near the royal palace at Tara. They lit a huge fire on the Hill of Slane to the north of Tara, and in the context of the story this was symbolic of the Biblical 'burning bush', as Patrick and his companions worshipped God in the full view of the forces of darkness. This was in direct defiance of the King who had decreed that no one could light a fire before he had done so. This act of deliberate confrontation could not be ignored by King Laoghaire, whose court was compared by Muirchu to the decadence of Babylon and King Nebuchadnezzar. The King and his retinue were aware of what Patrick represented, and concluded rightly that this fire of 'divine' origin was a threat to their way of life.

The King's druidical advisers warned him that unless the fire was put out immediately "it will never be extinguished at all." This was indeed to be a trial of strength which would determine the future of Christianity in Ireland. In Muirchu's story, the royal party took to their chariots and ventured out of the palace to take a closer look at this 'divine fire'. The King was strongly warned by his advisers not to approach the blaze, but Patrick was commanded by the royal party to step forward.

He did so, with confidence in God – and, according to Muirchu – with a psalm on his lips. The majority of the King's followers hurled abuse and curses at him, but he picked out the one royal retainer who believed in him, and blessed him. Patrick then prayed, and a druid fell down and was fatally injured when he hit his head off a stone. There was resultant darkness and an earthquake, and chaos ensued – in other words Muirchu's mighty account of the cosmic battle between good and evil did not lose anything in the telling.

St Patrick looks down from the Hill of Slane

The royal party retreated back to the palace in confusion, but the Queen wisely recognised the remarkable power which Patrick had demonstrated, and implored him not to destroy her husband. The King, in the meantime, had falsely promised to accept Christianity, but Patrick was warned about this by God. As he and his followers approached the royal party they were turned into the form of eight deer and a fawn and thereby escaped.

At this stage of the story there is a distinct parallel with Patrick's encounter with the Irish chieftain Daire in Armagh where he was reputedly granted the hill on which the present Roman Catholic Cathedral is built. However the King at Tara was made of sterner stuff, and he invited Patrick to a royal feast, where one of the druids tried to poison him.

Patrick, however, retained divine protection and he spotted the plot. When he blessed the cup, the liquid inside it froze, and when he turned it upside down the poisoned drop fell to the ground. Just to underline who was in charge, Patrick blessed the cup again, and the frozen liquid in the cup was turned back into its original form.

Despite this demonstration of 'divine power' the druids remained undaunted, and in a contest of 'magical powers' according to Muirchu, they tried every device to destroy

Patrick, but he thwarted all their efforts. Eventually the King himself gave up the struggle, and decided to accept Patrick's teaching with the words "It is better for me to believe than to die."

Patrick, however, was in no hurry to forgive his former adversary. He told the King that his rule would certainly continue, but because he had been so offensive to him and because he had so resisted Christian teaching "None of your offspring shall ever be king." In Muirchu's account of the confrontation, the moral was clear – "Oppose Christianity and Patrick's teaching at your peril!"

Whether or not all of this happened in the detail outlined by Muirchu, the story was a powerful example to later generations of the supremacy of God over the temporal powers. Indeed with the steady progression of Christianity, the power of Tara waned and the once-considerable jurisdiction of the High Kings of Ireland was no more. A statue of St Patrick, dating from the late-19th century, marks his 5th-century visit to Tara, and the epic confrontation between good and evil.

Today the Hill of Tara is peaceful and there are no echoes of the dramas of the past. Yet it remains geographically impressive and rises to some 300 feet, with a commanding

k at the Hill of Tara

view over a wide stretch of countryside – just exactly the right location for the ancient High Kings of Ireland. However there was another reason for choosing the Hill of Tara – as a Stone Age burial site it had a sacred significance long before the advent of Christianity.

There is still an atmosphere of this legendary history at the heart of Tara, with its hillocks and ridges, its Mound of the Hostages, its Bronze Age burial site, and its ancient stones. One of these – known as 'The Stone of Destiny' – was said to "roar in approval" when it was touched by the man rightfully destined to be King. Some people claim that Tara's distinctive identity may be under threat from a proposed new motorway, but it remains a considerable archaeological treasure-house, and an important destination for anyone who wants to touch the essence of Ireland's early history and also the St Patrick story.

LOCATIONS

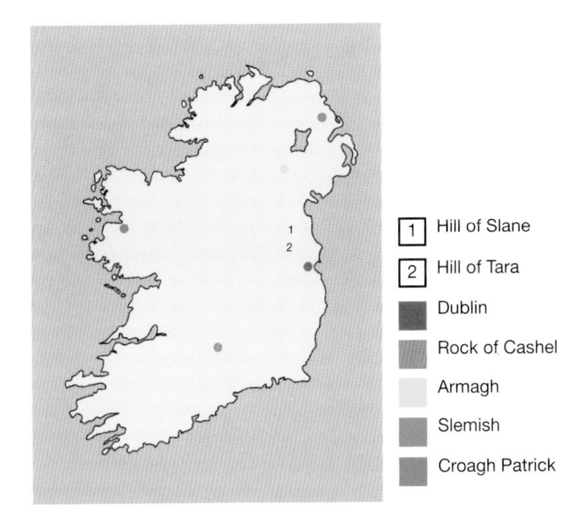

DIRECTIONS

Slane Hill is off the N2 (the main road from Dublin to Monaghan), just north from the town of Slane.

The Hill of Tara is accessible from the main N3 road from Navan, the largest local centre.

Rock of Cashel, County Tipperary

The magnificent Rock of Cashel in Co. Tipperary is associated with the area where St Patrick is believed to have baptised the Irish King Aengus and his son in the fifth century. This legend underlines Patrick's political astuteness, as well as his spirituality. He was fully aware that the baptism of local and national rulers would help to reinforce the establishment of Christianity in Ireland.

Indeed, he was not slow to use money to further his ends. As he noted in the *Confessio*, his 5th-century autobiography; "I spent money for you that they might receive me; and I went to you and everywhere for your sake in many dangers, even to the farthest districts, beyond which there lived nobody, and where nobody had ever come to baptise, or to ordain clergy, or to confirm the people. With the grace of the Lord I did everything lovingly and gladly for your salvation. All the while I used to give presents to the kings, besides the fees I paid to their sons who travel with me."

He continues later on "You know how much I paid to those who administered justice in all those districts to which I came frequently. I think I distributed among them not less than the price of fifteen men, so that you might enjoy me, and I might always enjoy you in God. I am not sorry for it – indeed it is not enough for me; I still spend and shall spend more. God has power to grant me afterwards that I may be spent for your souls."

Naturally, Patrick rejoiced in his converts, including those of high standing. He writes further: "Among others, a blessed Irishwoman of noble birth, beautiful, full-grown, whom I had baptised, came to us after some days for a particular reason: she told us that she had received a message from a messenger of God, and he had admonished her to be a virgin of Christ and draw near to God."

Given this authentic historical background to Patrick's earnest mission to convert the Irish, it is understandable that his name is linked traditionally to powerful figures like King Aengus at Cashel and his son. The legend of his baptism, however, is not without some painful humour. According to one version. Patrick in an excess of zeal drove his Bishop's crozier through the poor King's foot, but Aengus stoically suffered in silence. He remarked afterwards that he had thought this was all part of the ceremony of baptism as it reminded him of Christ's suffering.

The Rock of Cashel

Whatever the merits of this colourful story, there is no doubt that Cashel itself was for a long time at the centre of major power struggles in early Irish history. When Brian Boru became High King of Ireland in 1002, it was the signal for the beginning of a strong, though short-lived, central monarchy which the island badly needed after decades of disorder.

Brian Boru, having gained temporal power, then went to Armagh to receive spiritual approval from the centre where St Patrick had founded his first main church more than 650 years earlier. His supremacy was underlined by the wording in the *Book of Armagh*; "I, Mael Suthain, have written this in the presence of Brian, emperor of the Irish, and what I have written he has determined for all the kings of Cashel." This was, without doubt, a message to keep the ruling families of Cashel in their place.

Not surprisingly, however, after the death of Brian Boru at the Battle of Clontarf in 1014, the High Kingship passed back to Mael Sechnaill of Tara, until his death in 1022. It is no accident, therefore, that the traditional story of St Patrick is associated with such centres of political power as Armagh, Tara, Downpatrick, and also Cashel which remained the seat of the Kings of Munster until the year 1110.

On the Rock of Cashel, which towers magnificently over the plain at the edge of the town, are the remains of the strikingly beautiful 13th-century Cathedral of St Patrick which perpetuates his name – though there is no hard evidence that he actually founded a church there. Nevertheless his name has been linked to Cashel by tradition from the earliest times.

The Cathedral of St Patrick, with its soaring central tower and impressive chancel and nave, is indeed a worthy tribute to the great achievements of the saint himself. One of the most distinctive parts of this great complex of buildings is Cormac's Chapel, named after Cormac McCarthy, the former King of Munster, whose early 12th-century tomb it contains.

A museum in the Vicar's Hall, dating from the 15th century, displays a 12th-century St Patrick's Cross which used to stand outside the Cathedral. The spot is now marked by a replica. The museum also has 4th-century Coronation Stone which is believed to have been used in the coronation of successive Kings of Munster at Cashel.

Near the Cathedral there is a 12th-century Round Tower, which is still in good condition. This whole area exudes a sense of history, and there are numerous opportunities for good architectural photography – taking account of the Cathedral's dominance of the skyline. The Museum and Rock are open to the public all the year round, with seasonal variations. There is a good car-park nearby, and several attractive cafes and restaurants in the shadow of the Rock.

The cosmopolitan town of Cashel itself retains an air of history amid the bustle and affluence of modern Ireland, and there is much for the visitor to experience – including both a Roman Catholic church and a Church of Ireland cathedral. There is also the former Cashel Palace, now a hotel, the GPA-Bolton Library, founded in the mid-18th century, a Heritage Centre, the Cashel Folk Village which depicts the 19th-century town, and a reformed 17th-century peasant dwelling known as Bothan Scoir.

LOCATIONS

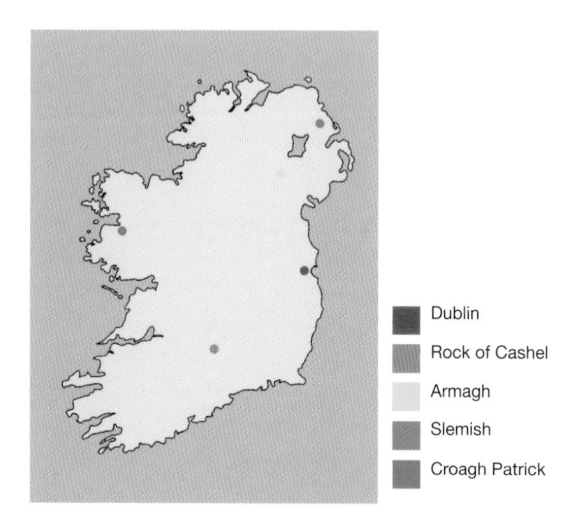

DIRECTIONS

Cashel is easily accessible on the main N8 road from Dublin to Cork, and several miles from Tipperary on the N74.

Ardagh and Clonmacnoise

The broad area of Ardagh and Clomancnoise in the midlands of Ireland and stretching to the Shannon estuary has connections with St Patrick and his successors. He was said to have established Christianity in Ardagh, and in Clonmacnoise are the remains of a 5th-century monastic site. This was part of the flowering of the 'island of saints and scholars' which was part of Patrick's legacy.

Though most scholars believe that Patrick's missionary journey took place in broadly the northern part of the country, he certainly claimed ecclesiastical authority over the whole island. This would add authenticity to the reports that he also made extensive visits to other parts of Ireland, or that his contemporaries did so in his name.

The church at Ardagh, for example, is said to have been founded as a wooden structure by Patrick's nephew Mel, whom he consecrated as a Bishop. The Ardagh Chalice, discovered in the mid-19th century, is a priceless artefact dating from the First Millennium. The original church built by St Mel has gone, but the town remains part of the important Roman Catholic diocese of Ardagh and Clonmacnoise.

High Cross at Clonmacnoise

HIGH CROSSES

One of the distinctive features of many Irish churches, graveyards and market-places was the erection of high crosses. One of the best examples in Ireland stands at Monasterboice, near the main motorway between Belfast and Dublin.

Monasterboice was a late-5th century monastic site of some importance, and reputedly established by a disciple of St Patrick's named St Buithe or St Boyce. Important historical structures remain here, including a 10th-11th century Round Tower, the Cross of Muiredach with sharp Biblical images, two other High Crosses and the ruins of two churches.

It retains the attractiveness of its mid-19th century Victorian layout with a Swiss-like sense of order, and one of the main buildings is the remaining structure of St Mel's Cathedral, with remnants from the 8th and 9th centuries. Ardagh is worth visiting because of its innate attractiveness and its connections with St Patrick and St Mel, but it should also be combined with a visit to the magnificent remains of Clonmacnoise monastery on the banks of the River Shannon.

This was founded in the mid-6th century by St Ciaran, and during its 600-year history it achieved a formidable European reputation as a centre of Christianity and

Monastic Site, Clonmacnoise

learning. The famous *Book of the Dun Cow* – relating to an animal that belonged to St Ciaran – is one of the earliest Irish manuscripts from Clonmacnoise which had a high reputation for Celtic art.

The ruins are extensive and impressive and include the Cathedral, several churches, Round Towers, a 13th-century castle and some 200 grave slabs. The 12th-century Nuns' Church was built by Dervorgilla, the wife of a local one-eyed King of Breifne called Tiernan O'Rourke who was abducted by the King of Leinster Dermot MacMurrough. Some people believed, however, that the lady had encouraged him to do so, and that subsequently his ardour cooled.

Meanwhile her offended husband decided to get even with the King of Leinster, and after a long and complicated story he took his complaints to France where they were heard by none other than Henry II. This reminded the King of his earlier intention to invade Ireland and it led indirectly to the Norman conquest of the island. The rest, as they say, is history. Perhaps if Queen Dervorgilla had spent more time in her church at Clonmacnoise the course of Irish history might have been different.

There are a number of important artefacts associated with the area, including the Crozier of Clonmacnoise which is

Grave slab, one of a collection on display at Clonmacnoise

now in the National Museum of Ireland in Dublin. The present Clonmacnoise complex retains a wealth of history, and it is an important stopping-place for those who wish to walk literally through an important part of the story of early Christianity.

LOCATIONS

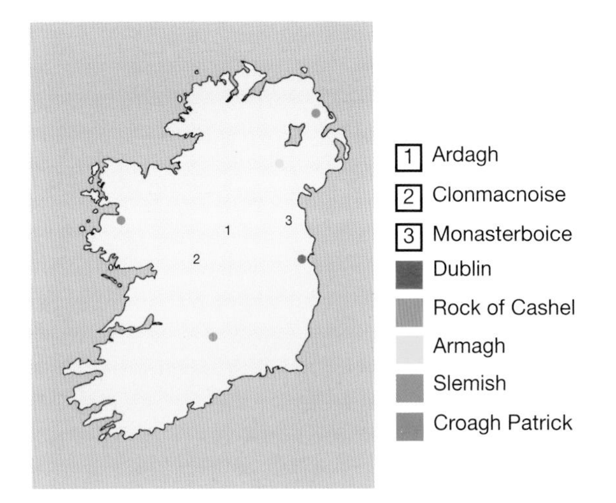

DIRECTIONS

Ardagh is 12kms off the N4 and S-E of Longford. Clonmacnoise is 21 kms from Athlone, signposted from N62. Monasterboice is 8kms north of Drogheda, off the N1.

Skerries, County Dublin

The legends about St Patrick are legion, and all of them colourful. One of these stories suggests that when Patrick first landed in Ireland on the Wicklow coast he was driven off by the natives. So he made his way to a small island near Skerries. This was renamed St Patrick's Island.

Luckily, he had been accompanied by a goat which provided him milk for sustenance on the island, and he grew fond of the animal. Periodically Patrick would leave the safety of his adopted island to sail to the mainland on one or other of his missionary journeys.

On one such occasion, people from the mainland travelled to St Patrick's island, and stole Patrick's goat. Unfortunately they later killed it for food. Naturally he was not best pleased on his return, and finding his goat missing, he literally strode across the sea to confront the people of Skerries.

At first they denied what they had done, but found that while they persisted with the lie, their voices were turned into a goat-like bleat. It was only when they told the truth that they recovered their voices. Even today Patrick's alleged footprint can be seen at Skerries, and in 1989

Sunset from Skerries, Co. Dublin

to mark the 50th anniversary of the foundation of the local St Patrick's Roman Catholic Church, the people commissioned a plaque depicting a goat's head.

With a fine sense of irony, the plaque was mounted inside the Church, thus giving back St Patrick his famous 'goat'. The inscription in Latin can be broadly translated as "That which was ours is restored on account of God and necessary friendship."

There is no known connection between this story, however, and the Irish phrase known as 'Getting My

Goat' – which refers to some person or situation which causes annoyance. Perhaps that's how Patrick felt when the native Irish literally 'got his goat' so long ago!

LOCATIONS

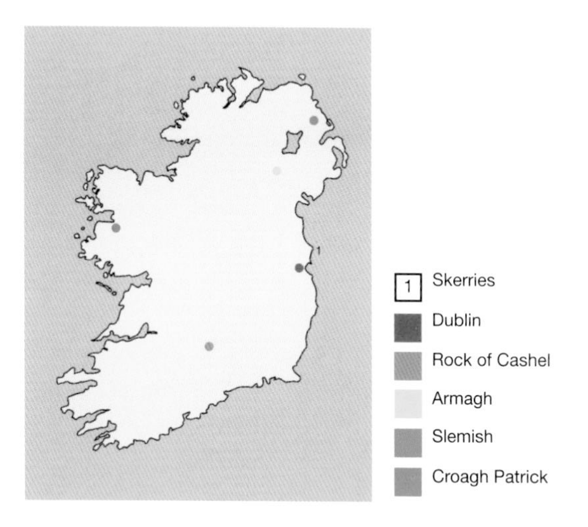

DIRECTIONS

Just south of Balbriggan off the N1, the main road north from Dublin.

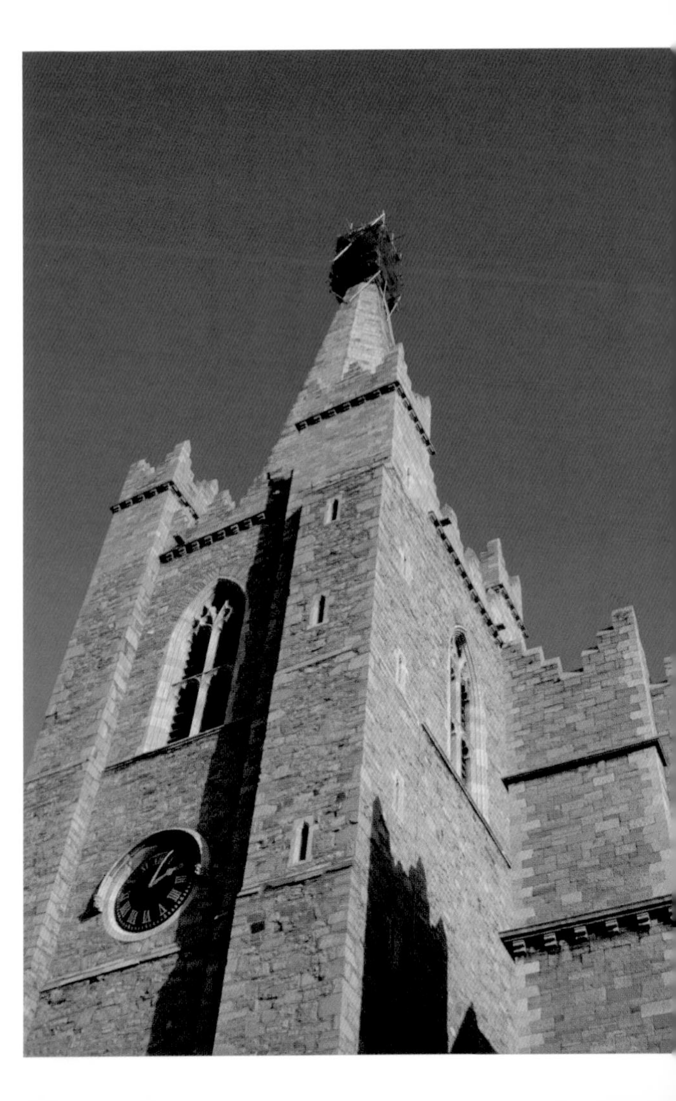

St Patrick's Cathedral, Dublin

The National Cathedral and Collegiate Church of St Patrick in Dublin is 91 metres long and nearly 18 metres high. It is Ireland's largest church, and is situated on a site where, according to tradition, St Patrick baptised converts at a well which formerly existed in a park beside the present building. A small wooden church was built nearby. From the 12th century the locals associated Patrick's name with an earlier church built beside a holy well.

This well appears to have existed until at least the 16th century, and in 1901 the site was rediscovered during excavations, when ancient houses were being demolished, and the spacious St Patrick's Park was being laid outside the Cathedral. A stone slab which covered the remains of the well was excavated and is now on display inside the Cathedral.

The association of this area with Patrick lasted down the ages, and on St Patrick's Day in 1192 the Normans consecrated a stone church on the site. In the early-13th century, between 1225 and 1260, this structure was rebuilt and dedicated. A Lady Chapel was also dedicated in 1270. In 1370 the west tower was reconstructed by Archbishop Thomas Minot after a fire, and in 1560 the first public clock in Dublin was placed there. A spire was added in 1749.

Situated on the south side of the inner city, the Cathedral has played a major role in the life and times of Ireland's capital. There is much to see in the historic building, and a detailed tour could take well over an hour, depending on the time available.

From the entrance at the south-west porch, there is the West End of the Nave, and its Boyle monument and two Celtic grave stones with Christian symbols – including the stone slab which covered what was left of the original well. The West Window, installed as part of the Guinness Restoration of 1864, has three panels, with 39 scenes from the life of Patrick.

Along the North Aisle are various historic artefacts and the white marble bas-relief of Turlough O'Carolan, the famous Irish harper, composer and poet who lived from 1670-1738, and "the last of the Irish bards." In the same area there is a small, attractive and modern statue of St Patrick himself by Melanie Le Brocquy.

In the North Transept there are some fine examples of Cathedral plate made in 1779 by the silversmith Richard Williams of Dublin. These are replicas of a silver chalice and flagon used by John Wesley, the founder of Methodism, during a visit in 1775. Four years later all the silver was stolen, and despite a reward of £100 – a good sum in those days – nothing was recovered. The Cathedral authorities asked Williams to craft a new set of plate, but at a cost not to exceed £112.

The distinctive Chapter Door records the history of a famous feud in 1492 between two powerful Irish families, the Earl of Ormond and the Earl of Kildare. Ormond's nephew 'Black James' had taken refuge in the Chapter House with his followers, and in an attempt to break the impasse, the Earl of Kildare himself cut a hole in the wooden door and reached through to 'Black James', as a brave gesture of reconciliation. He rose to the occasion, and grasped Kildare's arm instead of rejecting it. This is said to be the origin of the famous saying 'to chance your arm', in other words to gamble on the positive outcome of an enterprise.

Near the North Choir Aisle there is an inscription in honour of the distinguished Irish composer Sir Charles Villiers Stanford, whose music includes the definitive setting of the popular hymn 'St Patrick's Breastplate'. Across the aisle on the right there is a memorial to the Duke of Schomberg, one of the leading generals of King William of Orange whose Irish expedition at the end of the 17th century changed the course of British and Irish history.

Floor Tiles, St Patrick's Cathedral Dublin

There are various objects of considerable antiquity in the South Transept. These include two granite slab-crosses, dating from the 10th or 11th centuries, as well as two statues of a 'St Patrick' figure. One is wooden, and was given to the Cathedral in 1991 by two Co. Offaly sisters whose family had possessed the carving for generations. The other statue, in stone, was discovered in 1833 when rubbish was being cleared from the Cathedral. Unfortunately there is no certainty that either statue is genuinely Patrician.

In the South Aisle there are memorials to Douglas Hyde, the first President of Ireland, and Erskine Childers, the fourth President. There was a service in the Cathedral when Hyde, born in 1860 and the son of a Church of Ireland rector, was inaugurated as President in 1938, and his funeral took place here in 1949. Childers, who was born in 1905, became President in 1973, but, sadly, he died the next year.

Of particular interest in the South Aisle are the items commemorating one of the Cathedral's most famous incumbents – Jonathan Swift who wrote *Gulliver's Travels*, and other well-known works. He was Dean from 1713-45, and the pulpit from which he preached can still be seen, though it is no longer used. The tomb of this opinionated and accomplished author and senior church figure is situated in the South Aisle, and his self-constructed epitaph, over the door of the robing-room, has echoes of his turbulent career: "Here is laid the body of Jonathan Swift, Doctor of Divinity ... where furious indignation can no longer rend the heart."

Also on display are his bust, his death mask, a selection of his published writings, an imprint of his skull, and a parchment which awarded him the Freedom of the City, as well as the Queen Anne Warrant which enabled him to become Dean. Nearby is the memorial to his beloved friend Stella (Esther Johnson), and their graves are marked by polished brass plaques, side by side on the floor of the Cathedral. Dean Swift's observations have not lost their potency concerning

St Patrick's Cathedral Dublin

Irish life down the years – and not least that of 1728 when he wrote "We have just enough religion to make us hate, but not enough to make us love one another."

The ambience of the Cathedral is not that of an ecclesiastical museum – which it partly is, and gloriously so – but that of a living witness to the Christianity it espouses. As its very useful guide-book notes, St Patrick's "embodies the history and heritage of Irish people of all backgrounds from the earliest times to the present day. It continues the function for which it was founded – the daily offering of worship to Almighty God through the medium of great music."

LOCATIONS

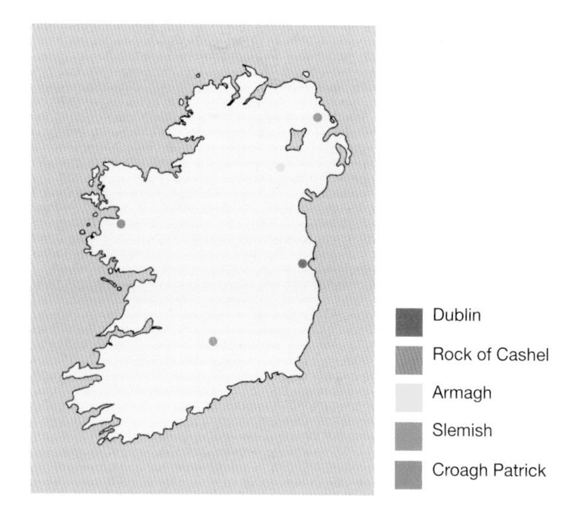

DIRECTIONS

The Cathedral is open weekdays throughout the year from 9am-6pm, though these times vary in winter. It is open on Saturdays from November-February between 9am and 5pm, and on Sundays from 10am-3pm. Various services are held daily, and visitors of all denominations are welcome.

Advance booking for groups is desirable. Guided tours are not provided, but guidebooks are available. Tour groups are not admitted during services, except for worship.

Parking for tour buses is available at St Patrick's Close. Wheelchair access is available by arrangement, preferably organised at least a day in advance. Toilet facilities are available. The bookshop is well-stocked and all proceeds are for the Cathedral's upkeep.

St Patrick's Cathedral is situated in St Patrick's Close, off Patrick Street in the Liberties area of Dublin.

Relics and Shrines

A number of the relics and shrines associated with St Patrick were an important aspect of Irish church life since medieval times, and a number of these significant artefacts are preserved in museums and private collections in both parts of the island. Some of these are connected with the development of the cult of St Patrick by Armagh from the 7th century onwards and to a lesser extent by John de Courcy around Downpatrick in the 12th century.

Relics of the saints, apart from their spiritual significance, were thought to contain healing properties, even in some cases for animals, and were highly-prized. They were also used for political purposes and promoted to draw attention to the so-called Church 'laws' of the saints. Those relating to Patrick were promulgated by Armagh clergy in the Provinces of Munster and Connaught in the 8th and 9th centuries. There was even a 7th-century Armagh text which stipulated fines for insulting the insignia of St Patrick.

ULSTER MUSEUM, BELFAST

Shrine of St Patrick's Hand
This distinctive object is currently on loan from the Roman Catholic Diocese of Down and Connor and has been on

Detail from a stained glass window, St Patrick's Church of Ireland Cathedral, Armagh

display in the ground-floor of the Ulster Museum. This is a hollow silver-gilt shrine which once contained a long forearm bone, thought to be that of St Patrick. The shrine dates from the 14th-15th centuries, and the base dating from the 18th century is displayed separately.

NATIONAL MUSEUM OF IRELAND DUBLIN

The National Museum in Dublin, adjacent to the Irish Parliament Buildings in Kildare Street, contains several important shrines and reliquaries of St Patrick.

Carving of St Patrick
This famous carving, dating from the early-6th century, was found in Faughart graveyard, Co. Louth. It shows Patrick treading on a large and lively-looking serpent, and lends weight to the tradition that the Saint "banished the snakes" from Ireland. This carving is located in the treasury exhibition on the ground floor.

St Patrick's Bell and Bell Shrine from Armagh
These are also located in the treasury exhibition on the ground floor of the Museum. St Patrick's Bell, which is plain and shaped like a cow-bell, is covered by an ornate Bell Shrine. This was made in the early-12th century in Armagh to preserve a much earlier bronze-coated bell which was believed to have belonged to St Patrick himself.

The Bell Shrine was traditionally used as a charm against diseases and other evils. It is ornately and beautifully decorated with silver and gold, but unfortunately some of the pieces were taken off for use as charms.

Shrine of St Patrick's Tooth from Athenry, Co. Galway
This purse-shaped artefact is located in the Museum's Medieval Ireland exhibition on the second floor, and dates from the 12th century, with repairs in the 1370s which were carried out by Thomas de Bermingham, Lord of Athenry. The Shrine was used at one time for curing sick animals, and when it was opened in the last century it was seen to contain a small lead cross and pieces of cloth. On the front there is a figure of the Christ, flanked by St John and the Virgin Mary.

Black Bell of St Patrick from Killower, Co. Galway
This dates from 7th-9th centuries AD and is also located in the Museum's Medieval Ireland exhibition on the second floor. This artefact is associated with the annual pilgrimage to Croagh Patrick, and is reputed to have been used by the Saint to banish demons from the mountain. Another version of the legend is that the bell's tarnished appearance is reputed to be reminiscent of the "fires of hell" when Patrick fought with the demons on Croagh Patrick. It is also thought to symbolise the victory of Christianity over paganism.

Incidentally there are a number of bells associated with St Patrick throughout Irish history but some scholars suggest that none of these can be directly connected with the Saint. However they are a vivid testimony to the rich legends surrounding St Patrick and his successful mission to establish Christianity in Ireland.

LOCATION OF OTHER MATERIAL

The Book of Armagh – Trinity College, Dublin.
Head Reliquary of St Patrick – Hunt Collection, Limerick.
Shrine of St Patrick's Jaw – St Malachy's College, Belfast.
Shrine of St Patrick's Thumb – Sienna Convent, Drogheda.

An American band taking part in Dublin's St Patrick Day Parade

St Patrick commemorated in New Hampshire

St Patrick's Day

This is celebrated throughout the world by people of Irish descent, and by everyone who enjoys a good party. It is a particularly popular event in places like the USA, Australia and Canada where there are many people of Irish descent, and also throughout Ireland itself. St Patrick's Day is also celebrated on the Caribbean Island of Montserrat, where a number of Irish emigrants settled after the Cromwellian prosecution of the native Irish in the 17th century. It is also, of course, a day of partying with the beer dyed green in America and elsewhere, and the copious consumption of dark Guinness and Irish whiskey. St Patrick's Day itself is as much a celebration of 'Irishness' as it is of Ireland's patron saint and in some ways St Patrick's Day Parades have as much to do with St Patrick as the legend of Santa Claus has to do with the true meaning of Christmas!

But it wasn't always so. Believe it or not it is only comparatively recently that St Patrick's Day parades were even organised in Ireland. The date of 17 March is important because St Patrick is thought to have died on that day, around the year 460 AD. In Ireland his death is still marked by morning church services in both the Protestant and Roman Catholic traditions. As a result St Patrick's

THE SHAMROCK

According to legend, St Patrick used the three-leafed shamrock as an early form of interactive educational device to teach the Irish about the Holy Trinity. It is a form of clover variously called *trifolium pratense*, *trifolium repens* or *trifolium dubium* and grows freely in Ireland, though not uniquely so. It is also found in Europe, from the Caucasus to Scandinavia, and in America.

The shamrock is the national symbol of Ireland, no doubt because of its Patrician associations. There is also a favoured Irish tradition of "drowning the shamrock" particularly on St Patrick's Day. This is self-explanatory, but there is also a surprising historical association with the British. It is thought that from the mid-18th century an extra ration of alcohol was given by English officers to Irish troops on 17 March, and they very sensibly "drowned the shamrock" in double-quick time. It is also said that Queen Victoria decreed at the start of the 20th century that Irish soldiers should wear shamrock on St Patrick's Day in memory of comrades who died in the Boer War.

St Patrick's Day in Oslo

Day has traditionally been treated as a Holy Day and pubs would keep to restricted Sunday opening hours.

There is another tradition that 17 March heralds the end of winter in Ireland. It was on this day, according to legend, that St Patrick took the 'cold stone' out of the water, which signalled that crop-sowing could begin. This tradition may also have had an association with pre-Christian times when important agricultural seasons were celebrated as part of the pagan calendar. The Christian Church may have taken these over for its own ends. Whatever the origin, there is still a saying in Ireland that St Patrick's Day

St Patrick's Day celebrated in Tokyo

brings 'the warm side of the stone' – in other words the ending of winter and the heralding of Spring.

The tradition of celebrating St Patrick's Day dates at least from the 7th century, but one of the first records of such celebrations being held outside Ireland is provided by Jonathan Swift, a former Church of Ireland Dean of St Patrick's in Dublin, and the renowned author of *Gulliver's Travels*. Writing in 1713 to his close friend Stella, he notes that on 17 March, the British Parliament was closed and that The Mall in London was so full of decorations that he thought "all the world is Irish". It is thought that the first recorded St Patrick's Day parade took place in 1762 in New York City, where there was a strong Irish immigrant population. This set a precedent for a whole range of similar celebrations on 17 March.

As Ireland itself became more secular and overseas visitors started to visit Ireland over St Patrick's Day the Irish very gradually started to hold their own parades as well. Now parades are held in various parts of Ireland and Great Britain, and many other places as well – with two of the biggest and best taking place in Dublin and New York. Others of note take place in Boston, Savannah, Chicago, Mississippi, San Francisco and other large American cities. St Patrick's Day is even celebrated in locations as diverse as Oslo, Tokyo, Manchester, Munich and many more as expatriate communities celebrate their heritage and the life of their patron saint.

St Patrick's Breastplate

The words of *St Patrick's Breastplate* were written by 'Patrick the Pilgrim' as he travelled to Tara in Co. Meath as part of his missionary outreach. In making his way to Tara he entered the territory of a hostile chieftain, Laoghaire MacNeill who laid an ambush for Patrick and his followers. As the group of pilgrims proceeded they sang a version of Patrick's prayer and were mistaken for a herd of deer and were allowed to pass by in safety. The words of the prayer were translated by the Irish hymn-writer Mrs Cecil Frances Alexander at the end of the 19th century. The hymn itself has nine verses and is worth hearing if you get a chance. The full version can be read in *St Patrick's Breastplate* also published by Appletree Press. Here is the best-known verse.

Christ be with me, Christ within me,
Christ behind me, Christ before me,
Christ beside me, Christ to win me,
Christ to comfort and restore me,
Christ beneath me, Christ above me,
Christ in quiet, Christ in danger,
Christ in hearts of all that love me,
Christ in mouth of friend and stranger.

Croagh Patrick where Patrick spent Lent

Acknowledgements

The publisher would like to thank the following for permission to reproduce work in copyright:

© Jaime C. Jordan (p 71);
© Eddie Mallin (p 76);
© Graham Alsop / www.flickr.com/photos/starbeard (p 82)
© Donal O'Cleirigh / www.istockphoto.com (p 88);
© Jessica Spengler (p 91);
© DUSI_BBG (p 104);
© Simon Jeacle / www.istockphoto.com (p 106);
© John S. Atherton / www.istockphoto.com (p 110);
© Jamie (Synaethesia) (p 112);
© Conor Nolan (p 120, top image);
© Lori Hurley (p 120, bottom image);
© Padraic Woods (p 123);
© Megan Walton (p 124);
© Annette Taylor (p 127)